# Bulletproof Title Due Diligence: Protecting Your Investments

By Alex Goldovsky

Whether you're a sophisticated investor or a beginner, this book will show you how to use title reports to guide purchase decisions of property, notes, tax liens or anything else involving title.

# CONTENTS

About the Author                                                          1

How I Started                                                             2

Introduction                                                             4

Chapter 1 – The Layman's Introduction to Title                          5

Chapter 2 – Understanding Deeds and Liens                               21

Chapter 3 – Mortgages and Notes Defined                                 27

Chapter 4 – Liens and Judgments Defined                                 38

Chapter 5 – Real Estate Tax Liens and Super Lien Basics                40

Chapter 6 – Real Estate Tax Liens – Advanced: Tax Sale and Tax
Deeds                                                                   43

Chapter 7 – IRS and Department of Justice Liens                         49

Chapter 8 – Home Owner and Condo Owner Association Liens                53

Chapter 9 – Municipal Liens: Surviving Foreclosure                      57

Chapter 10 – Municipal Liens: Water and Sewer Liens                     62

Chapter 11 – Bankruptcy Basics                                          67

Chapter 12 – Mortgage and Lien Priority                                 69

Chapter 13 – Exit Strategies: Foreclosure                               72

Chapter 14 – Exit Strategies: Deed in Lieu                              77

Chapter 15 – Alternative Investment Strategies: Contract for Deed 79

Chapter 16 – Chain of Assignment Breaks and How to Fix Them 81

Chapter 17 – Vesting and Origination Defect Risk Grading     85

Chapter 18 – Building a Due Diligence Platform     94

Chapter 19 – Building a Due Diligence Platform: 2nd Position Note Buyers     102

Chapter 20 – Building a Due Diligence Platform: Commercial Note Buyers     107

Chapter 21 – Common Issues for Real Estate Owned Buyers     112

Chapter 22 – How to Protect Your Portfolio Against Tax Sales     115

Chapter 23 – Curing Common Title Defects     117

Chapter 24 – Foreclosure Defense: Borrower Contested     121

Chapter 25 – Portfolio Risk Evaluation     126

Chapter 26 – Budgeting and Revenue Projection Notes     128

Conclusion     130

# ABOUT THE AUTHOR

Alex Goldovsky is founder and CEO of ProTitleUSA, a leader in nationwide residential and commercial title search, analysis and due diligence, servicing Fannie Mae, Bank of America, Wells Fargo, Colony, FDIC, SBA, First American and many others. His firm also serves individual investors, large and small. As of this writing, ProTitleUSA has been honored to make the *Inc. 5000* list as one of the 5,000 fastest-growing private firms in the country.

Mr. Goldovsky was the creator of a number of leading products in the title research industry, including an automated title exam and portfolio analysis dashboard for 1st position residential and commercial assets, exit strategy automation and many more. He is also a highly sought-after speaker at real estate investment and title-specific seminars and work groups, as well as a frequent guest on the *Price of Business* show and Bloomberg's *Home in Houston* radio show. He has a master's degree in engineering and holds nine U.S. patents.

Special thanks to Joshua N. Andrews, author of the book *Paper Profits: How to Buy and Profit from Notes, A Beginner's Guide,* who helped me edit the book.

# HOW I STARTED

A lot of people ask me how I became so successful in the title search business, an industry I hardly knew when I started. My answer: luck, desire, hard work, dedication, great employees and many other factors.

In the early 2000s, I was a marketing manager and program manager for Fortune 500 firms like Intel Corp, AT&T Bell Labs, Lucent Technologies, Conexant and others. But like many professionals at the time, I was a real estate investor on the side. I invested, with my wife, in university housing around the University of Delaware and University of Pennsylvania campuses, as well as in a commercial apartment complex in Philadelphia's Kensington section. The latter is a run-down, dangerous area about a mile away from up-and-coming Fishtown. I used a vendor for title search for my investments, but I never liked the level of service or results I was receiving. I knew enough to know that in Philly, the water, sewer and gas unpaid balances of a property would transfer from the prior owner to the new owner. The firm I was using was a nationwide firm and didn't seem to know the Philadelphia-specific issues.

When my first child, Roman, was three months old, drug dealers moved into my apartment complex. It was impossible to foresee, as the people who rented the apartment were on government social services, and had kids in their early teens; the kids were the drug dealers. I spent the next six months working with the Narcotics division of the Philadelphia Police Department, planning raids and kicking them out of my apartment building. When one day, I had a gun pointed at me by a gang member guarding the door, I was done. I sold all my real estate investments and focused on my new business idea – offering best-in-class title search services to investors nationwide.

I used my knowledge of online marketing, website building and program management to build a quality, accurate service, independent of property location. Sleep was a luxury in the first year, and I could not have built this business without the help of my lovely wife, Elena. She took over all of my responsibilities in the home and with my son. My close friends – Suren, George and Alex – taught me HTML, web development, Google online tools, virtual office setup and where to find all the resources I would need. I knew how to read the title search, but wanted to study everything relating to other states and counties. I read much online and ordered books from underwriters. And ProTitleUSA began to grow; today, (late 2017), we have 51 full-time employees, 1,500 contractors in the field and thousands of happy customers.

# INTRODUCTION

This book was written for the beginner to advanced investor – anyone who wants to learn how to invest in title wisely and safely, or grow their investment portfolio from one title to 1,000. On the surface, the title industry may not seem to be the most exciting subject for investors. However, understanding even the basics of title searches and how to read them can make or break any portfolio.

It is my hope that this book will provide a solid title education, show you how to create a bulletproof due diligence process and help you make better decisions about your investments.

Since we don't know each other (except for our shared interest in investing), I don't know how much (or how little) you know about this subject. So, we will start from the beginning. I will do my best to use layman's terms whenever possible, and to explain industry terms and meanings in an effort to make things understandable, clear and straightforward.

This book is meant as a primer, a collection of information to guide your decision making, and by no means contains all there is to know about title or title searches. I hope you will use it as such, and reach out to me or my team with any questions. With more than 25 years in the title business, it is likely that I have seen or heard of almost any situation you could possibly encounter.

# CHAPTER ONE

# THE LAYMAN'S INTRODUCTION TO TITLE

## Why Learn About Title?

Although I own and operate a company that focuses on title research, I am the first to admit that, for most people, this is a boring topic. It's a bit like studying bookkeeping or learning how to balance your checkbook – not exciting, but something that needs to happen, and which has real-world consequences if not done correctly.

As we go through this book, I will cover a variety of topics related to real estate title, and how the little details can affect your investments. These terms and ideas will apply directly to all types of real estate transactions, including residential fix-and-flip, buy-and-hold, commercial, land development, REOs, notes, hard money lending and more.

## What is Title?

What does the word "title" mean? In its simplest form, title can be summarized as a bundle of rights corresponding to a specific piece of real estate.

**According to investopedia.com, the definition is:**

"Unlike personal property, real property – such as real estate – is titled to convey ownership. This title must be transferred when assets are sold and must be cleared (free of liens or encumbrances) in order for transfer to take place. Unlike other real property assets, real estate ownership can take several forms, each of which has implications on how ownership can be transferred and can affect how they can be financed, improved or used as collateral."

We will discuss liens and encumbrances later in this book. But for now, the main takeaway is that title represents certain rights showing ownership interest in a property. This owner can be a person, trust, corporation or many other types of entities.

## Where Does Title Come From?

All documents which record the transfer of property ownership are stored and recorded at the county (or township, in selected states) recorder's office – the county where the property is located. All property information is accessible to the public, usually for a fee.

Whenever someone purchases a new home, sells a piece of property or otherwise transfers ownership, title documents recording this change are updated. Over time, this creates a string of records showing the very first owner of the property, and every subsequent transfer of ownership. This is the basis of title reports.

This report will show things like:

- property and ownership information
- property address
- APN or parcel#
- vesting information
- chain of ownership changes
- divorce, guardianship or probate transfers
- open or foreclosed mortgages
- mortgage-related documents
- active judgments or liens
- property tax amounts and if current
- property assessed value
- and much, much more

Of primary interest to the investor is that a title report shows the current owner(s) *and* includes others that may have a claim or interest in the property, including spouses, local taxing authorities, municipalities, etc.

The act of researching and reviewing these records in the recorder's office is called title research. After the research is complete, the finished work is called a title report. A title report is what you and I receive as investors, and what we use to answer many critical questions about our investment – preferably before we invest.

As you'll see later in this chapter, there are many different types of title reports. At the time of this writing, a report can range in cost from $49 to more than $200, depending on the property location and type.

## What Type of Report Do You Need?

There are several report types you can order and use, and you can also create custom reports. Many times, you don't need copies of all the records for a property; you may only need to know certain information in order to help you make an investment decision. This is where ordering the correct report matters.

Some of the common reports include:

### *Current Owner (Residential or Land)*

This report is ideal for foreclosure auctions, pre-tax auctions, short sales, tax sales, tax certificate purchases, note purchase transactions, by-owner transactions, refinances and checking for clear title. You will receive a title report on all outstanding mortgages, liens and judgments recorded against the property and the current owner(s).

**How and when to use it:** If you need to check all outstanding and unpaid liens, mortgages and judgments, and the tax status of the property, this is the report you need. It tracks all history from the last property purchase to the current date, as well as the vesting deed (person who currently owns the property).

## Mortgage and Assignment Search

This report is ideal for verifying the chain of assignments for any open mortgage.

**How and when to use it:** In many cases, the investor needs to determine who holds the rights to the mortgage against the property, based on the recorder's records, as well as whether the rights to the mortgage (recorded as assignment of mortgage) have any breaks in the ownership. Many document preparation firms use this report for preparing the next assignment in the chain, and servicers use it to verify that the mortgage has a clean chain before boarding the loan in the servicer system.

## State Statute Search (30-, 40-, 60-Year Searches on Residential or Land)

This report covers the following: chain of title search going back over 30 years based on the state statute, which can range from 25 years to 60 years; open mortgage and assignment search on all owners in the chain of title; federal, state and municipal lien information, as well as all owners in the chain of title; HOA (Home Owners Association) lien search on all owners; civil judgment search, including foreclosure proceedings; and tax delinquency status. All of the property-related information is captured on the State Statute Title Search summary page. This type of search also includes easements, restrictions and declarations that affect the property of interest. All relevant document copies are included in this service, including copies of all deeds in the chain of title.

**How and when to use it:** This search is a requirement for title insurance, real estate purchases, title opinions and evidence for a marketable title. If you are purchasing a property or ordering title insurance, this must be ordered.

The State Statute Search (sometimes called full search) is usually done when creating a title report for sale/resale transactions or for transactions that involve construction loans. It generally includes searches related to the following: property lien; easements; covenants, conditions and restrictions (CC&Rs); agreements; resolutions; and ordinances that will affect the real property in question. It will cover things like:

- Search for liens against the owner and the other parties on title
- Search for liens against the buyer (for sale transactions only)
- Search for bankruptcy and judgment proceedings against the owner of the property

## Two-Owner Report (Residential or Land)

This report is similar to the current owner report, but provides all copies of liens and mortgages vs. a list (an abstract of liens/mortgages). This will give you full documentation for all liens and a detailed transaction history. This level of information is not always needed, as many times you simply need to know what liens exist against the property, and the amounts.

The two-owner report is a great option for REO (real estate owned) properties, bank-owned properties and foreclosure auctions, where it's important to receive all copies pertaining to the title. Keep in mind that title reports of any kind will only show items which have been recorded at the county or circuit court level. Other agreements or liens may exist, but are less enforceable if not recorded. The reason? Whatever is recorded first has priority (to be discussed later in this book).

**How and when to use it:** This search is a requirement for foreclosure attorneys and REO buyers to verify which liens will survive the foreclosure, and will directly impact your investment.

### *Commercial Title Search*

Commercial title searches vary greatly by complexity and may be directed toward land development, commercial buildings, condo projects, cell towers, plants, environmental sites, oil and gas projects, or many commercial properties. Due to the complexity of commercial property title search, it's hard to fix the price of the search without initial review of public records and generating a responsible quote. In many cases, the cost of the commercial search can be the same as residential; however, the commercial search may be more complex and time consuming. Just like those for residential properties, commercial searches can vary in type from a current owner commercial search to a state statute commercial search.

Typically, a commercial title search includes a chain-of-title search covering all of the leases, mechanics liens and contracts that would affect the title on the property; open mortgage and assignment search; federal, state and municipal lien search; judgments search; and tax status. This type of search also includes easements, restrictions and declarations that affect the property of interest. All relevant document copies are included in this plan.

**How and when to use it:** Conduct a commercial title search f you need to check all outstanding and unpaid liens, mortgages and judgments, as well as the tax status of the commercial property by owner of the real estate. In the case of corporation or LLC ownership, this is also how you search for liens on known members or partners of corporate ownership structure. It tracks all history from the last property purchase to the current date, as well as the vesting deed (who currently owns the property).

## Foreclosure Guarantee Reports

A foreclosure guarantee is a type of report commonly used for foreclosing a lien on a property, like when a bank forecloses on a home. The title searcher will perform a full coverage search on the property in default, as well as a search for addresses of the lien holders. The addresses will be used for sending Notice of Foreclosure letters (such as Notice of Trustees sale) to all lien holders. This is a very specific report for foreclosure attorneys working with lenders, services or investors to represent them through the foreclosure process.

You can find more information at: protitleusa.com/PropertyReports.aspx

And at: wikipedia.org/wiki/Title_search

## Miscellaneous Report Types (A La Carte Selection)

There is a wide variety of property reports for real estate attorneys, lenders and title companies geared towards complex foreclosure title examination and interpretation. Those will not be a focus of this book, but I will mention some common types, as well as the specific purpose of each:

- **Update search (or bring down search):** Search for anything new recorded against the property or owners from the date of the last title search to current date

- **Chain of title only search:** 30-year chain-of-title or developer forward

- **Vesting deed search:** Based on the address provided, search uncovers the owner of the property and supplies a copy of the most recent vesting deed

- **Judgment-only search:** Used for uncovering liens and judgments against buyers in the county

- **HOA search:** To verify if the property is subject to any HOA dues and if there are any HOA liens against the property

- **Water/sewer search:** To verify the balance of utilities against the property

- **UCC secretary of state search:** To verify if the person or company has any liens registered under secretary of state

- **Tax-only search:** To verify the current status of real estate taxes against the property and report on delinquency of taxes, if any

- **Tax sale and redemption search:** To verify if the property is scheduled for tax sale of delinquent taxes, the date of the tax sale, redemption amount, last date to redeem and redemption process

- **Township search:** To verify any code enforcement violations or permit violations, or if subject property is scheduled for demolition

- **Second position mortgage search:** Used by second position note investors to verify if the second position mortgage is secured or unsecured against real property (more on this type of search later in book)

- **Bankruptcy search/scrub:** To verify if the bankruptcy was filed by parties on deed chain and if any mortgages, liens or judgments were removed by bankruptcy court from real estate title

- **Title exam:** We will help you interpret title search by means of a foreclosure report on any nationwide property determining and clearly showing the lien positioning, liens that remain with the property and liens that will be wiped out after the foreclosure auction. These reports are most valuable for lenders, foreclosing attorneys and foreclosure defense attorneys. They will determine the loan positioning, parties involved and who needs to be involved in the foreclosure process (with related document copies to provide the names and contact information), as well as examination of the 30-year chain of title to verify the ownership structure before or after the foreclosure auctions.

I understand this may be an overwhelming number of search choices, and you may even decide you need all of the above searches to make sure you cover all your bases. Don't worry; this book will help you with those decisions, based on your investment strategy. And if we work together through ProTitleUSA, I will help you make the best choice of products you need at the optimal price.

### *What Report Do You Need?*

Knowing which search you need will largely depend on what you need to know about the property. In most cases, you don't need to know who owned the property 50 years ago. You just need to know who owns it now, and if there are any liens or judgments on the title. Basically, you need to know exactly who has an interest in the property, and what amount of money or share of the property they may be entitled to.

When in doubt, just ask your title company for advice.

## Performing Your Own Searches

For the most part, anyone can perform a basic search, although in some cases you may need to physically visit the county recorder's office and/or pay county access and per-page copy fees. If you purchase real estate assets nationwide, of course, this becomes more difficult. The real question is, what is your time worth? If you are an active investor, pulling title yourself to save a few dollars is not a good use of your time.

An investor's time is best leveraged doing the following two items:

1. Locating and closing deals
2. Raising money to purchase more deals

Everything else – bookkeeping, accounting, title searches and non-income-producing items – should be outsourced to a qualified professional.

Allow me a quick anecdote: Sometimes I see highly paid business professionals mowing their own lawns. When I see this, it means one of two things:

1. They like to mow their lawn.
2. They don't value their time, and think they are somehow saving money by doing it themselves.

If you are a professional of any sort, your time is valuable, and you should never be performing daily activities you don't enjoy. So while you can generate your own title reports, unless you enjoy visiting the courthouse and trolling through reams of data and property histories, you should probably just have a title company pull the records for you. Trust me; it's worth the money.

## Speak the Title Lingo

There are a number of title-related terms that you must know to guide title companies to the product you need and to understand the title reports. Some terms are very important to understand in depth, not only to understand what is covered by a title report but also to take appropriate actions based on any alerts brought up by a title search. I suggest you take your time reading this section, and make sure you understand the material.

# The Effective Date

One important term you will come across in almost any title report is "Effective Date." This may also be seen as "County Index Date" or "Good Through Date." All three terms have the same meaning: the date of the last document visible to a title search company in the county recorder's office. This is not the date the title search was completed; if liens are reported before the date a report is completed and after the effective date of the county records, the title search will not show it. The difference between the date a report was completed and the effective date becomes a risk or unknown when you evaluate a property or a mortgage for your investment. To better understand what causes this issue, let's follow the process of how documents are recorded at the recorder's office.

# How Documents Are Recorded: An Example

Imagine you are buying a home. You have just completed the transaction and signed all the papers, and the bank has sent the money to the seller (assuming you have a mortgage). During the closing, you signed and dated the mortgage documents, including the deed and note for the property.

1.  Once the closing is complete, the signed documents are mailed to the county recorder's office. This includes other required paperwork, too, as well as a filing fee.

2.  After the documents are received by the recorder's office, they will be put in line behind other documents, waiting their turn to be filed. Remember, there are other people buying homes, too!

3.  The recorder reviews and approves the documents, then scans them into their computer system, a process known as "indexing." This means the documents are being compared

against the currently known property description using the legal description or parcel number as the identifier, to ensure they are recording the correct information on the right property. And yes, sometimes mix-ups happen.

4.  Once the documents are in the system, title search companies (and individuals) can view all documents related to the property, including the new legally binding mortgage documents you just signed. These documents (and many others) are reflected in title search reports.

As you can see, recording documents is a bit of a process, and not always a swift one. In addition, there can be a significant lag time between when things are sent to be recorded and when they show up on county records. This can create issues, because there could be valid liens and other problems hanging in limbo, waiting to be recorded, that a normal title search may not see. An easy way to protect yourself is to pull what is known as an "update service."

### Update Service to Cover the Risk

Update service is something any title company can provide for a nominal fee. It bridges the time gap from your last title report to the current index date in the county. It is not always needed, but it can provide peace of mind. Typically, the update service can be ordered if the initial title report was ordered within six months from the current date. As an example, for foreclosure auction property investors, the update service should be ordered a few weeks after the auction to make sure no liens were recorded right before the foreclosure sale that would hurt the investment.

# What is a Property's "Legal Description?"

Earlier, we touched on another important key phrase – "legal description." We don't need to delve into this too deeply, but it's important to know the basics because this is the method of description used on title searches and reports.

According to the American Bar Association, "legal description" refers to the written description of property and certain other data that identifies the subject piece of property. Since this definition is a little vague, I will describe three of the most commonly used methods of legally describing or identifying a property in the public records.

Most people are familiar with using street addresses as the best way to identify a specific property. The problem is that, over time, street names and landmarks identifying property locations can change. To remedy this, legal descriptions are used.

- **Fractional Designation:** The most common description, a fractional designation uses rectangular surveying to describe land in sections.

- **Metes and Bounds:** This form of description uses references such as streets and rivers to identify each point of the property (north, south, east and west).

- **Lot and Block Survey or Subdivision:** This newest description breaks land into plots or blocks to designate boundaries.

# What is a Property's Parcel Number?

Another property identifier commonly used is "parcel number." This is essentially a number assigned to a particular piece of property, usually by the county assessor or tax collector. It is also sometimes called the "Tax ID."

These methods of keeping track of property are different from the traditional physical address that you and I use on a daily basis. When you look at a title report (also known as a search), keep in mind it may not have the normal physical address listed. It may, in fact, use one of the previously mentioned methods to describe the property. You will want to verify that the address of the property on the report matches the property you are looking at. Sometimes there are errors; it's always smart to double-check.

## Documents Related to Real Estate, and Other Documents

Documents in the recorder's office are related to real estate property because they use the property's legal description as part of the content, or reference a vesting deed that describes the property in depth.

Two or more documents are related to each other if, in the body of the most recent document, there is a mention of older documents as a reference found in the county records in the form of Book, Page or Document Number.

When you look at an actual document recorded in the county, pay attention to the legal description referencing the subject property, the parcel number referencing the subject property and, finally, the property address (if any). Additionally, review any document references on each document and how they relate to one another.

### What is a Plat Map?

A plat map is a map filed by a developer (land surveyor) in the county records to show how the land is plotted in the subdivision.

### What Does "Unsecured Mortgage" Mean?

In this book, we will use the phrase *unsecured mortgage*. In title terms, it's a mortgage that can no longer attach to the subject real estate. The mortgage holder can only file for damages in civil court against the borrower, but never gain interest in the property. There are a number of events that may unsecure the mortgage, including a tax foreclosure deed, an HOA deed (in Nevada) and a bankruptcy court order.

## What Does "Chain of Title" Mean?

A chain of title is a collection of deeds to the property in chronological order to show how the ownership of the property changed hands through time.

## What Does "Chain of Assignments" Mean?

A chain of assignments is a collection of mortgage assignments against a property in chronological order to show how the mortgage ownership rights transferred from one lender to another, or one investor to another.

## What is a "Title Defect"?

Finding a title defect means there is an issue with the title search or title documents in relationship to your investment. Title defects can range from non-issues to severe. If you are a note investor and the mortgage was lost to a tax sale, this would be an example of a severe defect. If you are planning to foreclose on the property while the property was transferred from borrower to a land trust, this is a non-issue as it relates to your investment goal.

## What Does "Free and Clear" Mean?

The term *free and clear* is used when the property is not associated with any judgments, mortgages or liens.

## What is an "Exit Strategy"?"

Your exit strategy is your path to monetizing your investment. If you are buying properties at foreclosure auctions, generating rental income may be your exit strategy. Or maybe you will opt for a fix and flip. For note buyers (investors that invest in purchasing mortgages, rather than properties), your exit strategy may be as simple as reselling the note for a price that's higher than you paid.

## County Department Names and Roles You Should Know

When you invest in real estate, you have to know who holds the information you need, as well as their particular role within the county department regarding your property. Here's a quick primer:

- **County Assessor:** Maintains the legal description of the property, assigns a property parcel number in the county, assesses the value of the property (to be used to calculate annual taxes) and keeps track of the chain of title.

- **Treasurer or Tax Collector:** An elected official to the county office who collects tax payments from residents, maintains records of tax payments, reports delinquencies and typically administers the tax sales.

- **County (or Township) Recorder (or Clerk):** An elected official to the county office who maintains real estate records in the county.

- **Sheriff's Office:** An elected official to the county office who, on top of other functions, administers mortgage foreclosure sales in judicial states.

- **Clerk of Civil Courts:** In charge of filing judgments against the owner of the property – in a number of states, judgments are recorded in the civil court, not the county recorder's office.

# CHAPTER TWO

## UNDERSTANDING DEEDS AND LIENS

## What and Why

In this chapter, we discuss the differences between deeds and liens, and why understanding both is important for you, whether you're an investor, a noteholder or a real estate buyer.

## What Exactly is a Deed?

There is some confusion among beginning investors as to exactly what a deed represents. Does it mean you own the property? And if so, what happens to other existing liens, such as a mortgage?

A deed is legal title (ownership) of the property itself. This ignores the fact there could be any number of actual liens on the property. If liens exist, you will own the property "subject to" those liens. This means that although holding the deed grants you legal title and ownership of the property, there may also be liens which, at some point, will need to be paid or "satisfied." This typically happens when the property is sold or transferred to another party or paid off through regular payments like a mortgage.

A key thing to understand is that just because you hold the deed to a property, it does not mean you are directly responsible for any liens against it. The property itself is responsible. How can this be? Let's look at an example.

Let's suppose there's a property worth $300,000. You own a second lien mortgage on it for $50,000. But there's also a first position lien on the property for $200,000.

In this scenario, the property (and probably the borrower) will owe a combined $250,000. Let's suppose that you, as the second mortgage holder, are forced to foreclose on the home due to some unfortunate circumstances (and yes, you can foreclose on a home from a second mortgage position). After the foreclosure sale, you are given the deed to the home – you now own the property.

## So, What Happens Now?

When you completed the foreclosure on the second mortgage, that lien was extinguished, meaning it no longer exists. However, the first mortgage lien remains on the title. The first mortgage is still owed their money. In this example, you have three options:

1. Pay off the first mortgage in full.
2. Continue making payments on the first mortgage.
3. Don't pay the first mortgage – let them foreclose and, eventually, take the deed from you.

By owning the deed, you have effectively taken ownership of the property – subject to the remaining liens – which, in this case, is the first mortgage. This happens quite frequently and is not as complicated as it sounds.

## Common Deed Types

As mentioned, the document that shows the ownership transfer of a property is called a deed. Based on the type of ownership transfer, there can be different types of deeds. All convey ownership to another party.

### *Warranty Deed*

In some states, according to realtor.com, this is also called a Bargain & Sale Deed. Used in most real estate sales transactions, a warranty deed says that the grantor (previous owner) is the owner of the property and has the right to transfer the property to you. In addition, this deed serves as a statement that there are no liens against the property from a mortgage lender, the IRS or any creditor, and that the property cannot be claimed by anyone else. Title insurance provides the financial backup to the warranty deed, and requires a title search to verify that no other claims on the property are outstanding.

### Quitclaim Deed

A quitclaim deed is used when a property transfers ownership without being sold. No money is involved in the transaction, no title search is done to verify ownership and no title insurance is issued. This type of deed is most often used to transfer ownership within a family. The only exception is in Massachusetts, where the quitclaim deed may be used as a value transfer of the property.

### Sheriff's Deed

This type of deed gives ownership rights to property bought at a sheriff's sale, which is basically a foreclosure sale. A sheriff's sale is conducted upon the order of a court after a failure to pay a judgment or lien. In non-judicial states (more on this later), the foreclosure is held by the trustee and, therefore, the deed type is sometimes called a "trustee's deed."

Some states call this deed by a different name. Here are a few examples:

- In Florida, it's called a "Certificate of Title."
- In South Carolina, it's called a "Master-in-Equity Deed."
- In Georgia, it's called a "Foreclosure Deed."

(This will not be on the test.)

### Deed in Lieu of Foreclosure

When the property owner voluntarily transfers the deed (ownership) back to the lender instead of having the property foreclosed upon, a deed in lieu of foreclosure is used. This usually happens when the property owner knows they can no longer make the mortgage payments, or are in over their head. This can save the lender the time and money of a foreclosure, while helping the borrower save face – and sometimes their credit. It's important to note that the lender must voluntarily agree to accept the deed in lieu, as the borrower cannot just simply decide to deed the property over without lender consent.

### Tax Deed

This is a form of deed that gives authority for the property transfer free and clear of any liens to the treasurer of the county or township. This happens when the property owner does not pay the taxes due on the property. A tax deed gives the government the authority to sell the property, allowing them to collect the delinquent taxes and transfer the property to the new purchaser. In most states, a tax deed is classified as a "super lien," meaning it moves ahead in priority on the title. It can surpass even a first mortgage, and it's an easy way for the owner to lose their property. More on this in Chapter 3.

## What is a Lien?

Liens are very different than deeds. As discussed, a deed is actual ownership; a lien is a claim against the property or its owner for a specified amount of money.

If you have a mortgage on your home, you are familiar with a lien. The mortgage company gives you a mortgage loan in exchange for a lien against the property. This lien protects the lender in the event of default. The lien is an interest in the property; in this case, the exact dollar amount of the mortgage loan you borrowed. If you discontinue paying your mortgage, the lender may eventually foreclose using the legal rights outlined in the note and mortgage. From the sale of your home, the lender would only be able to collect the amount they are owed, plus any attorney's fees; not a penny more. Any extra money left over (if any) would go towards satisfying any junior liens (a subordinate debt, such as a second mortgage), then to the homeowner. The money left over from the foreclosure sale – called overage – goes to satisfy other liens.

A lien of any kind against a property will need to be satisfied or paid off before transfer of ownership or refinance can take place. The most typical transfer of ownership involves selling the property in some manner.

Remember, a lien holder does not own the property; the deed holder does. A lien holder only has a claim to the property for a specified dollar amount.

In addition to mortgage liens, there are many other liens (or claims) that are legally binding against a property. Some of these include:

- Real estate tax liens
- IRS liens
- HOA liens
- Mechanics liens
- Municipal liens
- Code violations

We will discuss these in more detail later.


## "First in Time, First in Right"

As you may imagine, and as you will see on many title reports, a property can have multiple liens against it. How do you decipher this information, and what does it mean for you as an investor?

Understanding title reports is complex, but there are some general rules of thumb you need to understand about liens and their recording order.

The first is a rule called "first in time, first in right." It establishes the priorities of liens recorded against a property. This rule states who gets paid, and in what order, in the event of a foreclosure or liquidation. In layman's terms, this means whichever lien was recorded first on the property title is in first position to be paid in the event of a default or sale. There are some exceptions to this, which we will discuss in later chapters.

In the event of a foreclosure or even just a regular sale, the priority of a lien matters. After a sale, the holder of the lien with the highest priority is paid first. Only after that party is made whole does the holder of the next highest priority lien receive any money from the sale. This continues down the list of liens until they are all paid – or until there is no money left. If there isn't enough money for all the lien holders to be paid, the holders of the lower (subordinate) liens simply don't get any money at all. Liens that were recorded before others have priority. This is what denotes a first lien, second lien, etc.

This is very important to understand, especially when buying notes or real estate. Depending on your business model, you will want to know exactly where your lien fits into the equation, as well as any other liens that may be damaging to your position.

When you see any lien on a title report, ask yourself three questions:

1.  **What type of lien is it?**
    Is it a mortgage lien, tax lien or something else?

2.  **What position is it in?**
    Liens recorded first have priority over other liens. This means that the very first lien (assuming it's still valid and unpaid) will be paid first in the event of a sale. Knowing the position of your lien on the title report is essential.

3.  **What date was it recorded?**
    Again, this goes back to determining your lien position. If you think you are buying a first lien, but see on the title report that it was recorded after another lien, then you really are buying a second lien. These details matter.

# CHAPTER THREE

## MORTGAGES AND NOTES DEFINED

*"A bank is a place where they lend you an umbrella in fair weather and ask for it back when it begins to rain."*
– Robert Frost

## What and Why

This chapter explains the basics of how mortgages and notes work. They are two separate documents that, together, legally secure a loan to a property. That property serves as collateral for the lender. I will also cover the differences between being a note owner and a landlord who owns property.

Mortgages are mentioned in English common law documents that date back as far as 1190. These documents illustrate the beginnings of the basic mortgage system as it still exists today. They describe how a creditor is protected in property purchase agreements. Specifically, a mortgage started out as a conditional sale where the creditor held the title to a property until the debtor could sell that property and recover the money paid.

What does that really mean for us today? Essentially, a mortgage is just a loan secured by a property. Most people don't have the liquid capital required to purchase a house in cash, so a mortgage helps them purchase a home they couldn't otherwise afford.

When a borrower approaches a lender to help him or her buy or refinance a property, that lender generates two legal documents: a mortgage and a note. These documents outline the terms of the loan arrangement and make it official. Then, to protect the lender in case of default, the transaction is recorded in the public records. A default takes place when an individual takes out a loan and does not pay as agreed. This could happen for a variety of reasons and does not necessarily make the borrower a bad person or a deadbeat. Most people who buy homes are hardworking, honest individuals, but sometimes they experience financial hardship – job loss, income reduction, illness or another unforeseen event – that prevents payment as agreed. Lenders need a way to protect themselves against these instances, however, and to recover their money in the event the borrower stops paying. This is why mortgages and notes exist as legal – but separate – documents.

### The Mortgage

A mortgage may also be called a "deed of trust," depending on the state where it originates. This document secures a lien against the property title in favor of the lender, securing the lender's interest in the event of default. This means if the borrower stops paying, the lender can legally foreclose – take ownership of the property – and sell it to recover the funds lent. Mortgage documents are recorded in public records and stay attached to a property until the loan has been paid in full or satisfied.

### The Promissory Note

A promissory note spells out the terms of the loan, much like an IOU. It outlines exactly how the mortgage is supposed to be repaid. The note will specify, in detail, items such as the repayment schedule, rate of interest, due date, any prepayment penalties and, ultimately, the date by which all funds need to be paid in full. In layman's terms, it is a promise to pay from the borrower. The note document may not show up on ordinary title searches.

When you hear investors talk about "buying a note," they are referring to both the mortgage and the note.

Another important point: When you purchase a note, you are not buying the property; you are buying all legal rights to the note and mortgage, which are really just pieces of paper. You are buying the borrower's promise to pay, as secured by their collateral (the property). This is a publicly recorded and legally enforceable IOU outlining terms and penalties for the borrower, as well as the legal remedies available to the lender, in the event of default.

In other words, you are buying the rights to an income stream.

## Basic Note Owner Rights

- To receive payments from borrower as outlined in the note and mortgage
- To sell or transfer ownership of the note to anyone, for any price
- To enforce the provisions of the documents, which include acceleration of the sums due in the event of default (remedies include foreclosure and/or selling the property)

## Rights a Note Owner Does Not Have

- They cannot physically enter or inspect the property
- They have no ownership of the property – that belongs to the borrower
- They cannot take any actions outside what is outlined in the note and mortgage
- They cannot change terms of the loan (a loan modification), unless the borrower agrees in writing

Most real estate investors are used to owning property. It's important to understand that, in this position, you are not the property owner. In many cases, from an investment standpoint, it's more beneficial to not be the property owner. This greatly reduces your liability and administrative burden. You don't need the headaches, hassles or midnight calls from tenants.

Just like with any other investment vehicle, one can focus on various niches in the market. As an investor, you can buy notes on virtually any type of property – secured or unsecured. Some examples:

- Residential (homes with one to four living units)
- Commercial (apartment complexes, strip malls, hotels, etc.)
- Mobile homes (single mobile homes or entire trailer parks)
- Raw land
- Automobiles
- Defaulted credit card debt

## Basic Terms to Know

### Performing
This is a note that the borrower is paying on time, as agreed. Usually the payments are monthly, but they can be based on any time frame depending on the loan terms.

### Non-Performing
This is a note where the borrower has stopped making payments and has entered into default. Many times, this was not the borrower's intention; it's often because they have fallen on hard

times. This simply means the note owner is not receiving payments as outlined in the note and mortgage. Often, this situation can be remedied through a loan modification or other remediating scenario.

### Re-Performing

This is a note that fell into a default situation where the borrower stopped paying. Then, usually through a loan modification or some other form of agreement with the lender, the borrower started paying again. You will hear this term used when the borrower has made at least six to twelve months of on-time payments and is current.

### Secured

This means the loan is secured by collateral – usually a home or property – which protects the lender. This is the best type of note to own, in my opinion, because if something unfortunate happens and the borrower stops paying, the note owner can enforce the terms of the mortgage and sell the property to collect most, if not all, of the money owed.

### Unsecured

This is a note with no collateral to back it up. The borrower still owes the money, but if they default, the lender has no collateral to sell to recoup the debt. This is a risky position to be in as a lender. I do not recommend ever buying unsecured loans, unless they are practically given to you or you have a highly specialized system in place for debt collection. There are large businesses that specialize in unsecured notes, such as credit card and consumer debt. These can be lucrative, but are not recommended for the beginner or intermediate investor.

### Unpaid Balance

This is also known as "UPB." It refers to the amount the borrower currently owes on a note. This does not include any arrears, missed payments or late fees that may apply. This ties into yield and discount calculations, which are discussed in chapter 10.

# Where Do Notes Come From?

There are three main avenues through which notes are created and enter the marketplace:

## Banks

When money is loaned on a real estate transaction, the lending bank creates a note and a mortgage (which may be called a deed of trust [DOT] in some states). The act of creating a loan is called "origination"" or "originating a loan." Many of these loans are later sold to downstream investors, especially if they become troublesome for the bank. This typically happens in a default situation, where the borrower has discontinued making payments. There are many good deals to be had for a private investor interesting in acquiring notes from a bank.

## Individuals

A common lending method that involves just the seller and the buyer is called "seller financing," and it can take many forms. The most common scenario is when Ma and Pa Jones want to sell a home they own. They would rather not worry about whether the buyer qualifies for bank financing, and are willing to act as the bank. Ma and Pa Jones are the sellers, and effectively become lenders to the buyer. The buyer gives Ma and Pa a down payment and then starts making payments to them each month, just like the buyer would to a bank. If structured properly, this can be a great benefit to all parties – Ma and Pa sold their home the way they wanted, and the buyer got the home he or she wanted. It's a win-win. A note and mortgage are still generated to document the transaction.

### *Private Lending*

Private lending occurs most often in the real estate investment world, and is often referred to as "hard money." People who provide private lending tend to prefer short loan terms – often one or two years, but they can be as short as six months. Private lenders have their own criteria for lending and prefer certain types of assets. These lenders are essentially investors or investment companies who have access to large amounts of capital and lend like a bank. Each time they lend, the money is secured by an asset, and it creates a debt for the borrower. Notes and mortgage documents are generated to document the transaction.

When viewing a title report, you will see any mortgages against the property. Take the time to examine these documents, as they contain important information which could affect your investment. Common items to examine for accuracy are:

- Recording date
- Signature date
- Book or instrument number
- Legal description
- Address or parcel ID
- Borrower's name
- Lender's name
- Trustee's name
- Principal amount (how much was initially borrowed)

## What is MERS?

During your title searches, you may run into an unfamiliar term, "MERS," usually on government or institutional transactions. Without going into too much detail, MERS stands for (according to Nolo.com, Mortgage Electronic Registration System, a company that was created by the mortgage banking industry. MERS maintains a database that tracks mortgages for its members as they are transferred from bank to bank. By tracking loan transfers electronically, MERS eliminates the long-standing practice that the lender must record an assignment with the county recorder every time the loan is sold from one bank to another.

The MERS system was created to help big banks simplify their transfer process when buying and selling mortgage notes.

## What are an Assignment of Mortgage and Allonge?

As you may know, mortgages and notes can be bought and sold, which happens quite frequently. Assignments and allonges are records of these transactions, and represent all past and current owners of the mortgage and note. It is like a chain of title, showing who has owned them in the past, who owns them currently and when ownership was transferred.

## Types of Mortgage-Related Documents

### Assignment of Mortgage
This is a document representing a change of ownership of the mortgage only. As you know, the mortgage and the note are two separate documents. When a lender sells the mortgage to another lender or the investor, an assignment of mortgage is executed and recorded in the county records, leaving a trail of ownership of the mortgage. Remember, we are talking about a bank or investor owning the mortgage, not the property owner.

The assignment will always have at least two parties involved in the ownership transfer:

- The assignor (the note seller)
- The assignee (the note buyer)

The assignment will also reference the original mortgage as part of the recorded assignment document it relates to, and includes information such as date of origination, recording date, origination amount and originating lender.

The legal description of the property may or may not be a part of the assignment, but should be in order to tie this document not only to the mortgage document, but to the property. An assignment document must be notarized and carefully prepared for recording, as it may be used as evidence in court during a foreclosure process. In short, the assignment of mortgage shows ownership of the mortgage itself.

## Allonge

This is a document representing a change of ownership of the note only. An allonge (from the French word "allonger," meaning "to draw out") is a piece of paper showing transfer of the note. It serves the exact same function as the assignment of mortgage, but for the note.

Why do we need two items to track ownership? Some people claim it's needed, but I find it redundant. Because the person or entity who owns the mortgage also owns the note, I see no reason to track things twice. Unfortunately, that's how it is done, and this document is still needed to prove ownership of the note.

## Release of Mortgage and Partial Release of Mortgage Documents

The purpose of the satisfaction or release of a mortgage document is to release the mortgage described in the document as it relates to the property and the borrower. Once the release is filed in the county records, the mortgage is not going to affect the real estate property. It's considered released.

There is also a common document called a "partial release of mortgage," which is designed to release a part of the property from the mortgage. To do so, it specifies the exact legal description of the released real estate in a *partial release of mortgage* document. Partial release of mortgage does not remove the obligation to pay the mortgage off; instead, it changes the real estate used as a security of the mortgage. In some cases, where multiple properties are described on the single mortgage, a partial release document may release only one of many properties under the same mortgage umbrella.

## *Substitution of Trustee, or Appointment of Substitute Trustee Documents*

A document important in non-judicial states is the substitution of trustee, or appointment of substitute trustee. The trustee has the power to foreclose on the property. When the mortgage is originated initially, typically a title company, title agent or mortgage agent is named as a trustee that "babysits" the transaction to make sure it goes according to applicable laws (TILA and RESPA, laws relating to disclosure). If the borrower defaults on the payments, the lender may choose a law firm to represent the lender in the foreclosure and name them a trustee for the mortgage, which is better suited for this function. To change the rights to foreclose from the old trustee to the new one, the substitution of trustee document is filed.

## *Subordination Agreement Document*

A subordination agreement is an agreement between the lenders on the position of liens against the property. Typically, the position of the lien is determined by recording the date of the lien, except when the lien holder voluntarily gives up the senior position through this agreement.

## Start of Foreclosure Documents: Lis Pendens or Notice of Default Documents

The lis pendens (in judicial states) or notice of default (in non-judicial states) is a document that constitutes the start of the foreclosure action by the lender or investor who is mentioned as a last assignee of record in the county in the assignment chain. There are a few states where the document is named differently or not filed at all. We will cover these states in later chapters.

## Final Step in Mortgage Foreclosure: Sheriff's Deed Document

To tie our discussion of the deed documents to mortgage foreclosure, the sheriff's deed would point to the final steps of foreclosure – the lender getting the property – while the lis pendens points to the beginning of the foreclosure process after the borrower defaults on payment of the loan.

# CHAPTER FOUR

## LIENS AND JUDGMENTS DEFINED

Liens and judgments are recorded in the county office, almost like the rest of the documents. By mentioning the legal description, property information or borrower/owner of the property, the liens or judgments may attach to both a property and borrower/owner of the property.

There are many types of liens that would exist against the person on the title and/or the property. This is an overview of the most common liens (we'll take a deeper dive into each category in future chapters):

- IRS liens are recorded in the county of primary residence against the person and are tied to each property owned within a county as a result of not paying federal taxes.
- US Department of Justice or USA liens are recorded against the person in the county of residence due to criminal penalties.
- Real Estate State Tax liens are recorded in a similar fashion as IRS liens, but for non-payment of state income taxes.
- HOA (Home Owner Association) or COA (Condo Owner Association) liens are placed against a specific property for not paying the home owners association dues.
- Tax liens reflect that the owner did not pay real estate taxes and the treasurer has placed a lien against the property.
- Mechanics liens can occur if the property is being renovated in any way (during the initial construction or later). The contractor may place a lien against the property for an unpaid amount toward the full invoice for labor.

- Sewer, Water or Utility liens are placed if the property owner does not pay for sewer or water.
- Code Violation, City or Municipal liens are placed if there are environmental or structural issues with the house or existing code violations.

Most of these liens can be dangerous to the investor because they can be a senior lien against the property, higher than the mortgage position. As I stated earlier, the details matter.

In addition to liens, a number of judgments may be placed against the borrower/owner in the county recorder's office, including credit card judgments, civil and personal judgments, judgments of foreclosure, judgments of divorce and foreign judgments (placed against the person in a different state or county and re-recorded in the county of residence). Most of these judgments, however, are considered a junior lien vs. a mortgage against the property.

# CHAPTER FIVE

# REAL ESTATE TAX LIENS – "SUPER LIEN" BASICS

Real estate tax liens (or, in short, tax liens) are the number one cause of investment loss to pre-foreclosure investors, REOs or note buyers. However, they're a gold mine for tax certificate investors (investors who pay taxes to the county on behalf of the owner in exchange for the right to collect interest until the tax certificate is paid, or the right to foreclose on the property for delinquent taxes).

## How Tax Liens Get Originated

Tax liens for unpaid taxes are sold to investors in 29 states, with some of the greatest sales activity occurring in Illinois, New Jersey and Florida. Local governments use property tax revenue to fuel the functions of public schools, police departments, parks departments, libraries and other vital local offices.

## Worst Case for Note Buyers

The selling of a delinquent property tax bill as an investment creates a *tax lien certificate*. An investor will pay the local government the amount owed in property taxes to the county (plus the interest due), thus creating a bridge loan. This allows the local government to continue its operations. In return, the county allows the investor to step into their lien position and charge the property owner additional interest. This is a first lien position and will trump the priority of a first lien mortgage in every participating state. Each state's tax lien statute varies slightly in the timeline, but after the investor has possession of the lien, the property owner must pay back the property tax debt with interest. If they are unable to pay, the investor has the opportunity to foreclose and take possession of the property at a fraction of its value.

As you can see, tax liens are serious business. If the property owner does not pay real estate taxes, the treasurer can auction off the tax lien, along with the right to foreclose on the property. Since a real estate tax lien is recorded in the county where the property is located, in the same way other documents are recorded, you should find any real estate tax liens in your title search report.

A real estate tax lien is a senior lien – often referred to as a "super lien" – and will not be wiped off by mortgage foreclosure, in most of the cases. This is why the savvy investor needs to pay the most attention to property taxes in all collecting jurisdictions for a subject property, as each collecting jurisdiction has the right to foreclose on the property – in the higher position than the mortgage or any other non-mortgage lien. (This is one of the key points in this book, so you might want to read that paragraph twice.)

## Multiple Jurisdictions Collecting

Sometimes property taxes are collected by multiple jurisdictions, and not just a county treasurer or tax collector. The property may be subject to township taxes, school taxes or personal taxes. In Pennsylvania, for example, there are always three tax jurisdictions collecting separately for each property – county, school and township. If your title search reports only county level taxes, you may be at risk of losing the property for unpaid school or township taxes.

## Tax Lien Naming

Tax liens reported by the county may take different forms in each state. The name of the recorded documents varies by state; for example, certificate of municipal sale in New Jersey, tax forfeiture in Michigan, and tax lien or tax deed in Louisiana. The names of these documents may be different, but they all state that real estate taxes were sold to a third party or forfeited to the treasurer.

## How to Read a Tax Lien

A tax lien document typically describes a tax certificate sale to the investor (purchaser of the certificate), including the amount paid for the tax lien at the auction, the annual allowed interest rate on the certificate (varies by state), and whether the treasurer reports that the taxes have been delinquent or sold as a standard tax status reporting of the treasurer (called a tax card). The tax card is not recorded at the county recorder's office; instead, it's maintained by the treasurer. Once an investor finds a tax lien in a title search, the very first thing that investor needs to do is to verify that it's against the property of interest. If the tax lien is a recorded document in the county records, verify that the legal description, address of the property and/or parcel number in the document matches the subject property. If the tax sale is mentioned through the tax card or tax status, verify that the tax card is, indeed, for the subject property by matching the legal description and parcel number. Once verified, the investor should raise the flag on the property to run further research and verify that the property is not scheduled for tax sale. If it is scheduled for tax sale, make sure you have enough time to redeem the delinquent taxes before it's too late and the investment is lost.

Besides the status of tax payment and recorded tax liens, the investor must understand the state law on how much time you have to redeem the taxes before they become unredeemable. Look for more details on this topic in the next chapter.

# CHAPTER SIX

## REAL ESTATE TAX LIENS – ADVANCED: TAX SALE AND TAX DEEDS

Before tackling this chapter, make sure you understand chapter five. If needed, read it again; I'll wait. We're about to take a deep dive into some of the advanced material on taxes.

If you are an entrepreneur like me, reading chapter five would most likely suggest that tax liens are a great alternative investment; a great method of making money. As I mentioned in the prior chapters, taxes are always the #1 position lien. They don't call them super liens for nothing. After a tax sale, when the treasurer is transferring the property to the new owner, the property is free and clear from all liens, including the mortgage. For that reason alone, investors have flooded the tax certificate and tax sale markets. After all, by paying cents on the dollar for taxes, you are getting a property.

## How a Tax Sale Auction Works

At a tax sale or auction, tax sale or tax certificate investors bid on the percent of interest they will be charging on a particular tax certificate or tax lien. For example, in 2010, an investor in Maryland was able to collect up to 12% interest on a tax certificate. In 2015, however, due to an overcrowded market, the interest rate in Maryland fell to 5-6%. The tax certificate market in 2017 was even more overcrowded, with the allowable interest rate for investors falling as low as 0-2%. Most of the tax deeds are ending up redeemed, making very little money for the investor in tax certificates. In a few cases, though, the owner or mortgage holder never redeemed the taxes on the property, which can translate into a lucky jackpot for the investor.

## How Much Time Do You Have to Redeem Taxes?

Here's a rule of thumb for note buyers: In most of the counties nationwide, the tax lien investor has to wait two or three years before applying for the tax deed. There are a few states, such as Indiana, Kentucky, Vermont and South Carolina, where the delinquent taxes can become a tax deed in little over one year after the sale of the tax certificate. Having a tax deed would constitute a final undisputed property transfer to the new owner (tax lien investor), with the exception of the states mentioned below with redemption periods after the tax deed is recorded.

## What Is the Best Approach for Catching Tax Issues?

If you are a beginning investor buying a few loans, I always recommend calling the treasurer yourself and asking these questions (I will explain the reason for these questions later):

1. Are the taxes current? And are there any delinquent taxes on the property?
2. Who pays the taxes? The tax lien investor or the lender/escrow company or borrower?

These questions have been carefully crafted to give you the information you need. Question #1 will tell you if the treasurer has all taxes current. In other words, the treasurer does not care who pays the taxes, as long as they are completely paid. This question will flush out anything outstanding tracked by the treasurer. Question #2 will tell you about the entity paying the taxes, possibly raising a red flag if the tax certificate buyer keeps paying consecutive years of taxes.

# Properties in New Jersey – Be Careful!

New Jersey is known for reporting the taxes as current while the investor is paying taxes. The treasurer will always answer the question the way it's presented – nothing more, nothing less. For example, if you ask the treasurer if there are any delinquent taxes, the treasurer will answer "No; everything is paid and current." Unless you ask who is paying those taxes, you may be in for the unpleasant surprise to find out that the taxes are being paid by the tax certificate buyer in, say, 2006, and that the tax certificate buyer has been paying consecutive years of taxes, charging the maximum interest rate allowable by the state. In fact, what makes New Jersey unique is that New Jersey townships sell three types of municipal liens through township tax sales – sewer/water, common change and tax liens. Sewer/water and common change liens are treated as regular municipal liens (to be discussed in later chapters), but tax liens can be very dangerous for the investor.

As mentioned before, when the tax deed is recorded in the county records, the property may still be redeemed in the few states below.

# States with Tax Deed Redemption

If you invest in foreclosed properties or mortgage notes, take notice if you see a tax deed on your title search; this does not automatically mean that the mortgage or property is completely lost to tax deed or tax foreclosure. There are two types of tax sales. The first type is when the treasurer issues a tax deed directly at the tax sale auction. The second type is when the treasurer issues a tax sale certificate, enabling tax certificate investors to file for the tax deed in the form of an application once the redemption period expires. In most cases, the second type, once recorded, is not redeemable. With the first type, however, the investor can redeem the tax deed before the transfer of property becomes final and unredeemable. The table below may give you guidance on the tax deed redemption time for the states that record redeemable tax deeds.

| State | Tax Deed Redemption Period | Comments |
|---|---|---|
| Arkansas | 30 days after tax sale* | |
| Connecticut | 6 months | |
| Delaware | 60 days | |
| District of Columbia | 6 months | |
| Georgia | 1 year | |
| Hawaii | 1 year | |
| Louisiana | 3 years | |
| Maine | 2 years | |
| Massachusetts | 6 months | |
| Minnesota | 1 year | |
| Montana | 60 days | From the deed application date |
| North Dakota | 3 years | |
| Pennsylvania | 9 months | Only applies to Philadelphia, Pittsburgh and Scranton |
| Rhode Island | 1 year | |
| South Carolina | 1 year | |
| Tennessee | 1 year | |
| Texas | 2 years | 6 months for non-homestead |
| Vermont | 1 year | |

# Know How Fast a Tax Certificate Can Become a Tax Deed

It's important for the investor to understand the time period left to pay off taxes before there is any danger of losing the mortgage or property to a tax sale. The table below gives a state statute view for states with non-redeemable tax deeds. The middle column shows the quickest time the tax certificate buyer can apply for a tax deed, wiping off the mortgage after the tax certificate purchase or tax delinquency in years. The right column shows whether states record a tax certificate in public records or keep track of delinquent tax years by the treasurer on a tax card (TC Tax Certificate or Tax Forfeiture; DEL Delinquent tax years required before applying straight to tax deed).

| Tax Certificates with Potential for Tax Deeds | Years after Tax Certificates (or Delinquency) to Tax Deed | Type |
|---|---|---|
| Alabama | 3 | TC |
| Alaska | 2 | DEL |
| Arizona | 3 | TC |
| Arkansas | 2 | DEL |
| California | 5 | DEL |
| Colorado | 3 | TC |
| Florida | 2 | TC |
| Idaho | 3 | DEL |
| Illinois | 3 | TC |
| Indiana | 1 | TC |
| Iowa | 1.75 | TC |
| Kentucky | 1 | TC |
| Maryland | 2 | TC |
| Michigan | 1 | TC |
| Mississippi | 2 | TC |
| Montana | 1 | TC |
| Nebraska | 3 | TC |
| Nevada | 2 | DEL |
| New Jersey | 2 | TC |
| New Mexico | 3 | DEL |
| New York | 2 | TC |
| Oklahoma | 2 | TC |
| Oregon | 3 | DEL |
| South Carolina | 1 | TC |
| South Dakota | 3 | TC |
| Utah | 4 | DEL |
| Vermont | 1 | TC |
| Virginia | 3 | DEL |
| Washington | 3 | DEL |
| West Virginia | 1.5 | TC |
| Wisconsin | 2 | DEL |
| Wyoming | 4 | TC |

In later chapters, we will use the material covered here to create a method of evaluating taxes on large portfolio assets or loans, a bulletproof due diligence workflow system designed to catch every tax-related issue involving a property or asset.

# CHAPTER SEVEN

# IRS AND DEPARTMENT OF JUSTICE LIENS

IRS liens, a result of not paying federal taxes, are recorded in the county of primary residence of the property owner, and are tied to each property owned by that owner within that county.

An IRS lien has a special 120-day redemption provision after the chain of ownership event. After the 120-day redemption expires, the IRS lien becomes a junior lien. For investors in foreclosed properties, this event of ownership change is a foreclosure deed. This would mean that the IRS lien would "cloud" the title for the period of 120 days after the foreclosure.

In cases where the investor wants to resell the property before the 120-day redemption expires, the IRS allows them to request a petition for property release.

Below is an example IRS response to the request to partially release the IRS lien from the property, but not the prior owner. In this example, the IRS agreed to release the property that the investor foreclosed on with negotiated payment as a smaller amount than the face amount of the lien. The investor who foreclosed on the property then needs to apply for a partial release of the IRS lien, providing the IRS with the deed to the property showing the ownership change, amount of funds agreed upon and final settlement documents (if the transaction was not a sheriff's sale or trustee's sale).

Department of the Treasury
Internal Revenue Service
**IRS** Small Business / Self-Employed Division
955 S. SPRINGFIELD AVENUE
2ND FLOOR
SPRINGFIELD, NJ 07081

Date: MAR 1 7 2016

Person to contact:
████████████

Employee ID number:
████████████

Contact telephone number:
████████████

Contact fax number:
████████████

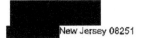
New Jersey 08251

This letter responds to your application for a Certificate of Discharge of Property from Federal Tax Lien under Internal Revenue Code (IRC) Section 6325(b)(2)(A).

☒ We approved your application. We are enclosing Letter 402 or 403, as applicable, which is our written commitment to issue a certificate of discharge as soon as we receive the documentation we requested in the enclosed letter.

☐ We denied your application because you haven't met the requirements for discharge under the IRC section shown above. You can appeal this determination through the Collection Appeals Program, as explained in the enclosed Publication 1660, *Collection Appeal Rights*, and Form 9423, *Collection Appeal Request*. If you want to appeal our decision, contact the person listed above as soon as possible.

☐ Additional information about the denial, if applicable:

☐ We need more information before we can approve or deny your application. Specifically, we need the documentation listed on the attached sheet within  days from the date of this letter. If we don't receive this information within that timeframe, we will close your request without appeal rights.

# US Department of Justice (DoJ) Liens

Department of Justice liens, or USA liens, are recorded against the person in the county of residence due to criminal penalties. The Department of Justice is less willing to negotiate than the IRS.

Based on my experience, once verified that it's against the borrower by Social Security number (SSN), a DoJ lien will attach to the property based on the percent of ownership. The fact that your title search found the DoJ lien puts you, as an investor, on notice of its existence. These liens are also frequently called government superior liens. For example, if the DoJ lien is against the husband, and the property is owned by the husband and his wife as joint tenants, the DoJ lien will attach to 50% of the property. As the Department of Justice does not negotiate well, they typically ask for the full amount as a payoff. They are also capable of freezing assets under Asset Forfeiture regulations, creating a cloud over the title, with the worst outcome being forfeiture to the government. You can, however, negotiate with the prosecutor to allow the foreclosure sale to continue and have this cleared. The prosecutor then must determine whether the proposed forfeiture of a residence serves a compelling law enforcement interest based on the following criteria:

- The nature of the underlying criminal activity being facilitated by the residence;
- The extent to which the property was used to facilitate or conceal the underlying criminal activity, including such factors as the amount of time that the property was used, the frequency of such use and the total portion(s) of the property used in facilitating or concealing the underlying criminal activity;
- Whether the perpetrator or any other persons involved in the underlying criminal activity have an ownership interest in or reside at the residence; and
- If the owner of the residence is neither the perpetrator nor otherwise involved in the underlying criminal activity, whether he or she would likely prevail on an innocent owner defense.

An investor with an interest in the property at the time the illegal activity was occurring can defeat the government's proven forfeiture claim by establishing one of the following:

- Investor did not know of the conduct giving rise to the forfeiture; or
- Upon learning of the conduct, the investor did all that reasonably could be expected, under the circumstances, to terminate such use of the property, including (1) giving timely notice to an appropriate law enforcement agency of information that led the person to know the

conduct giving rise to a forfeiture would occur or has occurred, and (2) in a timely fashion, revoking permission or making a good faith attempt to revoke permission to those engaging in such conduct to use the property or taking reasonable actions in consultation with a law enforcement agency to discourage or prevent the illegal use of the property.

Investors who acquired an interest in the property after the illegal conduct occurred can also defeat the government's proven forfeiture claim by establishing that they qualify as a bona fide purchaser for value of the interest and that, at the time they acquired the interest, they did not know, and were reasonably without cause to believe, that the property was subject to forfeiture. When the evidence available before filing a civil forfeiture complaint demonstrates that the likely owner of the property was either the perpetrator or a knowing participant in the activity, that evidence should be sufficient to overcome any "innocent owner" defense.

As you can see, a Department of Justice lien is a little bit more involved, but can still be removed if handled properly.

# CHAPTER EIGHT

# HOME OWNER AND CONDO OWNER ASSOCIATION LIENS

A Home Owner Association (HOA) lien can wipe off the mortgage in Nevada by HOA Foreclosure and recently, as of the writing of this book, Massachusetts became the second state that can wipe off the mortgage in the same way.

HOA (or COA, Condo Owner Association) liens can be dangerous to investors in certain states known as super lien states. The HOA lien is put on the real estate property for unpaid common charges and home association dues. There are 22 super lien states where an HOA lien is considered a higher priority lien than the mortgage, making it possible to foreclose on the property out of position. The priority of the HOA or COA lien is established by the recording date of the condominium declaration and bylaws documents in the county records (in other words, when the homes were built), as compared to the recording date of the mortgage. If HOA dues are not paid, the HOA can file a foreclosure action against the property and foreclose on the property. Some states do not require an HOA to put a lender on notice when recording the start of a foreclosure action. Some super lien states also allow the HOA or COA to collect attorney fees, which can add up to thousands of dollars – on top of the HOA delinquent dues.

In October of 2014, the Nevada Supreme Court confirmed that the HOA foreclosure completely wiped off the first position mortgage, making the title free and clear. The ruling became a wake-up call for investors, lenders and servicers to search for a market solution for monitoring HOA liens against the properties or assets in current lender portfolios every year or six months, which represents the shortest time for an HOA to foreclose on a property. My recommendation, if you own an asset in one of the super lien states, is to have a proactive lien monitoring solution in place.

(See table on page 60 for super lien states.)

In non-super lien states, HOA and COA liens are less dangerous; however, they always attach to the property described on the HOA lien recorded document and would need to be paid off for the title to be free and clear. In fact, an HOA lien would survive the foreclosure, but not the tax sale. A tax deed would also wipe off the HOA lien from the property title.

## Paying Off the HOA Lien

The difficulty in paying HOA liens is figuring out whom to contact for payoff. In many instances, the management company representing the HOA, or the HOA itself, files a lien in the county records, making it more difficult to find the contact for payoff. An HOA typically has a board of directors consisting of a few residents in the same development. Adding to the challenge, each member of the board of directors is re-elected every 2-3 years, so your contact information may become obsolete at the lien filing. To make it easier for lenders, there are companies dedicated to tracking any and all changes in the board of directors for each HOA in United States.

Luckily, an HOA lien will have contact information for the attorney's office representing the HOA, so if that office represents the HOA in the lien or foreclosure action, the names of the board members may not matter.

If you are at a complete loss on where to find the HOA information on a given property, contact the local realtor for listings of properties in the same development.

## Paying Off the HOA Balance

In a number of states, the HOA balance (not yet a lien) must be paid off at the time of the foreclosure by the lender. Many investors or lenders pay the face value of this balance, although some investors are successful in negotiating the payoff. My suggestion: negotiate first, pay last.

# Negotiate an HOA Pay-Off

The sooner you, as an investor, start the HOA lien negotiation, the less chance you have for the HOA lien to hurt your investment in the future. You may want to request to be contacted if the attorney representing the HOA starts a foreclosure. Remember, you must be an official interest holder in the property (by assignment of mortgage, if you are a note buyer, or by sheriff's deed, if you buy properties at foreclosure sales) to be properly serviced for states that require servicing to interest holders. Once the assignment of mortgage is recorded into your company's name, you become an interest holder. Make sure that the address and contact information of the assignment is accurate, so other parties may contact you.

# HOA Restrictions on Investments

This may be a little off-topic, but worth mentioning: For note investors whose primary exit strategy is mortgage foreclosure and putting a rental tenant in the property, it's important to review the HOA declaration document or its amendments to verify that there are no legal restrictions for renting the property after the ownership transfer. I know of an instance where an investor foreclosed on a property and put in a tenant. After a few months, the investor received a large fine from the HOA for violation of Condo Declaration and was requested to evict the tenant. This case is a great example that the HOA is not only able to post a lien for non-payment of HOA dues, but also to record an HOA Declaration Violation that can result in significant loss.

**ProTitleUSA**
Nationwide Title Due Diligence

| | HOA Super Lien States | HOA priority over Mortgage (UCIOA) | UCA States | HPRA States | Standalone | IS HoA Attorney Fees and FC Cost Secured? | Notice to Lender Required? |
|---|---|---|---|---|---|---|---|
| AL | Yes | | | | | No | Yes |
| AK | | Yes | | | | No | No |
| CO | | Yes | | | | Yes | Yes, upon request |
| CT | | Yes | | | | Yes | Yes |
| MN | | Yes | | | | Partially, depending on who pays the HOA | No |
| NV | | Yes | | | | No | No |
| WV | | Yes | | | | No | No |
| MD | | | | | Yes | No | Yes, upon request, along with filing of lien |
| PA | | | Yes | | | No | No |
| RI | | | Yes | | | Yes – fees and costs limited to $7,500 | Yes. Failure to send notice removes attorney's fees from super-priority lien |
| WA | | | Yes | | | No | Unique requirement – notice by lender limits superpriority period to 3 months; prior notice from assn to lender maintains 6 month period |
| DC | | | | | Yes | No | No |
| FL | | | | | Yes | Depends | No, but Recordation of lien is required |
| MA | | | | Yes | | Yes | Yes, to eligible mortgagees |
| NJ | | | | | Yes | No | Yes, along with filing of lien |
| OR | | | | | Yes | Yes | Yes |
| DE | | Yes | | | | No | Yes |
| VT | | Yes | | | | No | Yes |
| TN | | | Yes | | | No | Yes |
| HI | | | | Yes | | No | Only on demand |
| IL | | | | | Yes | No | No |
| NH | | | | | Yes | Yes | Yes |

# CHAPTER NINE

## MUNICIPAL LIENS: SURVIVING FORECLOSURE

City or township liens that are outstanding against the property are called *municipal liens*. Municipal liens are considered a superior lien, and always have a higher position than the mortgage. This means that, in the case of a mortgage foreclosure, municipal liens will survive and need to be paid off by the property owner or lender.

As mentioned in prior chapters, not all liens are recorded in the county recorder's office where the property is located. Most townships or cities have departments that keep permit and code violations records for all properties within the city/township limits, and that's where many municipal liens are found. Typically, the department responsible for keeping these records is called the Code and Compliance Department or the Permit Department.

## From Violation to Demolition: An Example

If not resolved within the allotted timeframe, municipal liens may also cause the property to be scheduled for demolition. In this example, I'll show you how a city puts a fine against a property, which then could lead to demolition.

A homeowner, Mr. White, rebuilt his house without a city permit and took out a construction mortgage that you are planning to buy as a note investor. The city found out that the construction took place without a city permit and labeled the property as an unsafe living structure. They slapped a fine or issued a permit violation on the property, then scheduled regular inspections to verify that the issue was being resolved, during which time the fine continued to accrue interest. Suddenly Mr. White moved out, leaving the property vacant. He also stopped paying the mortgage, taxes and utilities. The city filed a suit against Mr. White to fix the permit violation or they would have the right to demolish the building. Since Mr. White was gone, no one contested the order, so the city scheduled the property for demolition.

Since property demolition lists are kept at the city or township Demolition Department – with nothing yet recorded in the county office – you, as the investor, might be completely unaware of the impending demolition. In some cases, the city will have a record of the suit in the civil courts, but a common investor mistake is buying a note without making a call to the township offices; it's not always possible to see these types of issues through a title search report alone.

The demolition scenario is rare, but it happens. ProTitleUSA, in fact, has many townships and cities as clients and most of them (but not all) are required to notify interest holders in the property when a demolition will be taking place. But, whether you are a beginning investor or a large asset fund, you must realize the risk and either be diligent in your research, or be prepared for the occasional write-off.

In my experience, code violations and demolition searches are usually afterthoughts in the due diligence of asset portfolio acquisition. It's a surprise to many that most code violations, as a rule, are not recorded at the county and most likely will not appear on the title report, since they are tracked and recorded by cities and townships at the city hall level. The city of Jacksonville, Florida, for example, has a separate code violation department which keeps a database of violations not appearing in the county records. In New York, the Environmental Control Board (ECB) and Department of Building (DOB) violations are not recorded in the county records, but tracked within each individual department by the owner's name, property address and/or legal description. The danger to the investor comes when these violations become enforceable liens against the property in the form of the municipal lien or a tax lien.

## Department of Building Violation: An Example

One of the large hedge funds bought a note based on the title report alone, which did not include a search of the Environmental Control Board (ECB) and Department of Building (DOB) violations in the city of New York. After the note purchase, the DOB lien was converted to property taxes and assumed a higher lien position over the mortgage the client bought, costing them a lot of money. (The vendor they used was not ProTitleUSA, by the way; we always include Environmental Control Board [ECB] and Department of Building [DOB] violation searches in properties located in New York boroughs, as we know how frequently this happens.)

I was an investor myself, so I always look at every situation from the investor's point of view. I know what's at stake, and I want to know that all of our bases are covered. It's almost impossible for any single investor to understand all the nuances of municipalities across the country. It took ProTitleUSA about seven years to become experts in these differences and be able to help investors uncover these hidden dangers.

## Comparing Photos to City Violations: An Example

An apartment building had a hole in the roof that made the property unlivable. The city posted a note on the property door to fix the issue by a certain date, or they may decide to consider the property for demolition. In most of these instances, the property is vacant, so that note on the door probably stayed there a while. During your due diligence process, as an investor, you ordered an external BPO (Broker's Price Opinion) with pictures of the outside of the property. Your BPO vendor sent an experienced broker or appraiser to take pictures of the property, including close shots of the door and, hopefully, a view from above. When you saw the front door of the property and the hole in the roof, you saw the posting, and began to compare the condition of the building to the municipal liens and violations. In this example, seeing the note on the door raised a red flag that the property may be scheduled for demolition – and saved you from a big financial mistake.

## Advice to Investors

If you are buying a single note for a house purchase, be diligent. Don't skip the step of calling the township to speak with the department responsible for code violations and demolition. Make sure the property or note will not suffer the devastating scenarios described in the examples above.

If you are buying a large number of assets, ProTitleUSA offers support for a code violations and demolition check as an additional service to streamline your due diligence process. We are built for volume and can process municipal searches – thousands at a time.

Here are a few state-specific examples for my readers who may be thinking, "I want to know exactly which municipal liens stick to the property." If you are reading this book for general education purposes, however, feel free to skip to the next chapter.

### New York:

> ECB (Environmental Control Board) building code violations can turn into tax liens. The official policy language is: Notwithstanding any provision of law to the contrary, one or more environmental control board judgements against an owner for a building code violation with respect to a private dwelling, a wooden-framed single room occupancy multiple dwelling or a dwelling with a legal occupancy of three or fewer dwelling units shall constitute a tax lien on the property named in the violation with respect to which such judgment or judgements was (or were) rendered, as hereinafter provided. Such liens shall be entered and enforced as provided in this section.

### Illinois:

> A lien for unpaid garbage and debris removal services will not be eliminated upon completion of a mortgage foreclosure. This is because it is superior to all prior existing

liens, except taxes, if it is recorded within 60 days after the removal costs are incurred.

A demolition lien will not be eliminated upon completion of a mortgage foreclosure because it is superior to all prior existing liens, except taxes, if it is recorded within 180 days after the completion of the demolition work.

A certificate sold by a receiver in a building code violation case will not be eliminated upon completion of a mortgage foreclosure. This is because it is superior to all prior existing liens, except taxes, if the certificate holder records the lien within 90 days of the transfer from the receiver to the holder.

A lien for the extermination of pests such as rats or termites will not be eliminated upon completion of a mortgage foreclosure. This is because it is superior to all prior existing liens, except taxes, if it is recorded within 60 days after the extermination costs are incurred.

## Texas:

A municipal health & safety lien (for mowing, brush clearance, rubbish removal or any other city-ordered work to remedy an "objectionable, unsightly, or unsanitary matter") attaches on filing of the city's lien statement with the county clerk, inferior only to tax liens and liens for street improvements.

A municipal demolition lien (for securing, repairing or demolishing substandard buildings) attaches on filing and indexing of the city's lien statement in the office of the county clerk. This lien is a privileged lien subordinate only to tax liens.

# CHAPTER TEN

## MUNICIPAL LIENS: WATER AND SEWER LIENS

More than most, this lien type is typically misunderstood or unknown – water and sewer liens and balances. Water and sewer liens typically survive a mortgage foreclosure; however, this is not set in stone. The priority of a water and sewer lien is determined by a local jurisdiction law (not federal or state). You may have one township in the state that puts water and sewer liens above mortgages in priority, while another township in the same state will consider water and sewer liens junior to mortgages. To make matters more complex, some jurisdictions will make water and sewer liens an outstanding balance attached to the property. In other words, the water and sewer outstanding balance might attach to the property and you, as an investor, would never know about it.

Water and sewer liens are the most common types of municipal liens. Unfortunately, as mentioned previously, the attachment of utility liens is not federally regulated; instead, the local municipal government creates regulations that would affect your investment on a county-by-county or even township-by-township basis. Typically, public utility liens don't foreclose on the property as a superior lien. At the same time, utility liens, in many cases, will survive a foreclosure and attach to the property.

When you foreclose on a note and are about to record a sheriff's deed to gain possession of the property, the recorder will require you, as the investor, to pay off all outstanding balances for public utilities before recording the deed into your name. The payoff amount can easily be a few thousand dollars, which, of course, would greatly affect your ROI (return on investment).

# The Utility Lien Priority Rule of Thumb Approach

If the water/sewer/gas utility lien is recorded in the county with the plaintiff being the local jurisdiction, liens will attach to the property. If the lien is filed by a third-party provider, it can be assumed as a junior lien.

If you are doing your due diligence on a nationwide real estate asset or note purchase, below are a few examples of the different state regulations across the country. Again, if you are reading this for general education purposes, skip to the next chapter.

## California:

When unpaid charges are added to the assessment on real property pursuant to Water Code section 36726 and filed with the tax collector, they are automatically secured by a lien on the land pursuant to Water Code section 36825. The lien of the assessment has the same priority as the lien to secure real property taxes and, therefore, takes priority over private liens. The district's lien remains intact regardless of the foreclosure action, and the purchaser takes title subject to the lien.

After the filing of all parts of the assessment book with the tax collector, the assessment on each parcel of land is separately assessed and any penalties for delinquency added thereto, plus any unpaid charges for water and other services added to the assessment under the provisions of Section 36726, is a lien on the land and impart notice of the lien to all persons.

## Illinois:

A lien for unpaid water and sewerage services will be eliminated upon completion of a foreclosure for all counties, except Cook County, providing that the county shall have no preference in any such lien over the rights of any lien holder arising prior to the notice of filing of such lien. Be aware, however, that despite the lien's foreclosure, the municipality may still refuse to provide water or sewer services to the property until the outstanding charges are paid. Cook County requires a complete water and sewer pay-off to record the deed.

The city of Chicago requires a Full Payment Certificate (FPC) for all transfers of real estate. An FPC is a certificate issued by the Chicago Department of Finance indicating that all water and sewer charges and penalties that accrued to a water account are paid in full or otherwise not transferable to the subsequent owner. A completed FPC application serves as a request to the Department of Finance to transfer service out of the transferor's name and into the transferee's name. Without an FCP, the parties will not be able to obtain the Chicago Real Property Transfer Tax stamps, which are required to record the property deed with the Cook County Recorder of Deeds. Unless otherwise provided by law or rule, an FPC is required in all transfers of real property, whether such transfers are subject to or exempt from the Chicago Real Property Transfer Tax.


## Michigan:

Unpaid water and sewer bills are certified as liens in November of each year and turned over to the tax collecting authority for collection on March 1. Once turned over to the tax authority, an unpaid water/sewer bill becomes a delinquent tax.

**New Jersey:**

In New Jersey, as in other states, property owners are legally required to pay property taxes on their holdings, and to pay other municipal charges for which they may be liable, such as sewer and water charges, special assessments, or liens for abating nuisances such as boarding or removing debris from the grounds of a property. All these liens are known as priority liens, because they have priority under the law over other liens, such as mortgages and judgments.

If a property owner fails to make timely property tax payments, the property may be subject to tax foreclosure, either by the municipality or by a third party who has bought the tax lien from the municipality.

**Ohio:**

Water and sewer liens must be paid off to get the transfer deed recorded.

**Pennsylvania:**

The water, gas and sewer balances are lienable only in Philadelphia County, but not in other counties.

In Philadelphia County, water, sewer and gas balances are lienable against the property. These utilities also take first position when a property is sold at a foreclosure sale (when the property is sold, the proceeds are used to pay the city utilities first; what is left goes to the bank, who will be in the second position). If any money is left after the bank is satisfied, it will go towards paying off any debts below the bank's position or to the ex-homeowner.

## Texas:

A municipal utility service lien can be imposed by city ordinance for unpaid water or other utility services provided by the city, and is attached on recording of the city's notice of lien in the local real property records. This lien is inferior to a bona fide mortgage recorded prior to the city's lien, but is superior to all other liens, including previously recorded judgment liens and any liens recorded after the municipality's lien.

## Washington:

If you do not pay the water bill for your home that receives water/sewer service, that unpaid bill can become a lien on the home. That lien, if not paid, can be foreclosed upon. The relevant statute states that a water/sewer district may claim a lien for the unpaid balance, and that the unpaid balance shall be a lien against the property upon which the service was received, subject only to the lien for general taxes. The lien is given greater priority than even a mortgage. This lien is second only to general property taxes.

This rule applies even to a home with renters leaving an unpaid water bill. In short, if the renter does not pay the unpaid bill, the homeowner is stuck with it. This is not the usual policy for other utilities like cable or electric services.

# CHAPTER ELEVEN

# BANKRUPTCY BASICS

When you buy a real estate asset, you must run a bankruptcy search on the property's owner. As the investor, you must know whether or not the owner is in active bankruptcy, or you cannot proceed with any foreclosure. Let's cover the flow of bankruptcy filing basics.

When a borrower files for bankruptcy for financial protection, it's typically done for the purposes of removing unsecured and/or second position liens. Any foreclosure action or tax sale is put on hold until the borrower is discharged from bankruptcy. The bankruptcy court sets up a new fictional entity called a "bankruptcy estate," and this entity has the power to transfer the property from the owner to other parties in the effort to pay off the debt declared in the bankruptcy proceedings. In almost every instance, the bankruptcy cannot remove the first position mortgage. However, the lender and borrower may execute a mortgage modification agreement while the borrower is in bankruptcy to lower the monthly payments for a certain period, giving time for the borrower to catch up on the payments for the remainder of the secured debt. Some investors in notes in bankruptcy think this is very beneficial to them, that the bankruptcy court forces the borrower to cooperate with the lender within the court framework rather than chasing the borrower outside of court to sign modification agreements. In fact, in this case, lender and borrower both win.

Junior (second, third, etc.) position mortgages or judgments may be stripped off in bankruptcy, becoming unsecured liens through the judge's order "to strike a junior lien." From the title search perspective, bankruptcy search is a must-have verification of which liens, judgments and mortgages were stripped by a bankruptcy order. It should be a part of your standard note or property due diligence not only to verify if the second lien was stripped, but to also find out if any of the unsecured judgments were removed through a bankruptcy proceeding.

Bankruptcy is really a widely discussed and popular topic. The borrower can use bankruptcy to remove any unsecured debt, such as credit card, personal judgments or junior position liens, while the first position lender can benefit from bankruptcy to force a favorable modification with the borrower ordered by a judgment with a very strict payment plan. Once the borrower pays the modified amount for a period of six to nine consecutive months, the price for the performing note/asset will be much higher than the price for a non-performing note before the bankruptcy.

## Hidden Danger for Investors

We have seen a few bankruptcy cases where the attorney representing the borrower in bankruptcy sneaked the discharge of the lien into the restructuring plan for the borrower. If the lender is not well represented or not careful with bankruptcy case handling or review, the judge may approve the plan with the order to strike a lien. There is no reverse action that the lender can take to undo this chain of events.

# CHAPTER TWELVE

## MORTGAGE AND LIEN PRIORITY

## Worth Repeating: A Mortgage Lien Priority Recap

For the beginner note investor looking into first position notes, lien priority is the most important concept to understand; it determines the priority of all interest holders in the property with respect to collecting their interest. In other words, lien priority determines the order of debt collection against the person or the property. It's also the first thing we look at when evaluating risk on any note purchase.

If we only refer to mortgages, a secured debt by real estate property, the priority of a mortgage is determined by the recording date of the mortgage. The earlier the recording date of the mortgage, the higher the priority of the mortgage lien against the property. If two mortgages are recorded on the same day, the priority is determined by the earliest instrument number (or book and page of the recording). For example, if the first mortgage was recorded on 01/01/2000 for $10,000 in Book 5, Page 1, and the second mortgage was recorded on 01/01/2010 for $1,000,000 in Book 5, Page 25, the $10,000 mortgage is considered in the first position, and the $1,000,000 mortgage is in the second position.

Of course, this is an unlikely example, but it can happen. This is considered an origination error where the title company who recorded both mortgages committed an error and now you, as an investor, have to resolve this priority error by filing a document called a subordination agreement. This is the only way to make sure the priority of the lien stays with the higher mortgage.

## Involuntarily Lien Priority

In some cases, liens are placed against a person or property without approval of the owner/borrower; they're called involuntary liens.

Real Estate Tax liens (the result of unpaid or delinquent taxes) are considered, in most cases, first priority liens that supersede even mortgages. Any municipal lien, city lien, environmental lien or sewer/water/utility lien (in some states) is considered a higher position lien than the mortgage, as well. HOA liens are considered a higher priority lien over the mortgage only in two super lien states (Nevada and Massachusetts). In rare cases, mechanics liens may be a higher priority than the mortgage. The only scenario where a mechanics lien is a higher priority than a mortgage is when the lien states that the materials (goods) delivered to the property arrived earlier than the recording date of the mortgage. The common example is when the property is new construction and the owner is taking out a mortgage on the purchase at the same time as the builder is supposed to release (pay to all contractors) all mechanics liens.

## Liens that Cloud the Title

IRS, Department of Justice (DoJ), USA and state tax liens are considered liens that cloud the title. In the prior chapter on IRS liens, we pointed out that the IRS has a 120-day redemption period after the event of the ownership change, which clouds the title for the period of 120 days before an investor can resell the property. State tax liens are typically junior to the mortgage if they're recorded after the recording date of the mortgage. SBA (Small Business Administration) mortgages in the junior position have a one-year redemption from the event of the change and, for the investor, an SBA mortgage on the title would mean that the property cannot be sold for the period of one year.

## Some Common Terminology

A senior position lien assumes a higher lien priority than the subject mortgage. A junior position lien assumes a lower priority than the subject mortgage. Junior liens don't survive subject mortgage foreclosure, while senior liens do.

The main reason lien positioning is important is the direct impact it has on estimating the total cost involved in perfecting a first lien position for first lien note investors. If there is a municipal lien found against the property, and the goal is to get a clear title, the lien must be paid off, as it would survive the foreclosure.

## Perfecting a Lien Position

Another term you might hear as you invest is "perfecting lien position." If you are buying a note and your title search comes back with various senior liens, you can make your subject lien a first lien by paying off those liens or forcing other parties to file satisfactions of senior liens. If this is your course of action, you are perfecting your lien position.

# CHAPTER THIRTEEN

## EXIT STRATEGIES FOR THE NOTE INVESTOR: FORECLOSURE

Mortgage foreclosure is considered a common exit strategy for note investors. As a general rule, once the borrower defaults on mortgage payments, a first position mortgage gives you the right to file a foreclosure action against all lien holders to gain possession of the property for the purpose of reselling it. The foreclosure process takes anywhere from eight months to one and a half years, depending on the property's county and state. Many investors use foreclosure as a last resort when all other options fail.

Let's touch on the relevant documents used in a foreclosure case. You will understand why it's important to become familiar with these documents later in this chapter.

## Foreclosure-Related Documents

To ensure legal processes and procedures are followed correctly, each foreclosure case is typically filed by an attorney representing the lender. The beginning of this process is easy to recognize simply by looking at a title search report and seeing the documents commonly filed at the start, middle and end of a foreclosure. In judicial states, the foreclosure attorney files a lis pendens document in the county records at the start of the foreclosure action. In non-judicial states, the lender may file one or two documents at the start: 1. A substitution of trustee document to transfer the right to foreclose on the property to the attorney chosen by the investor or current note holder, and 2. A notice of default document to begin the foreclosure process. If the foreclosure case is dismissed or inactive, both documents have their associated documents filed to cancel the foreclosure action – the release of lis pendens or release of notice of default.

In many cases, when investors are buying mortgage notes and running title due diligence, the presence of these documents would tell you how far in the foreclosure process the attorney is on the subject property, therefore potentially providing additional savings on the foreclosure costs compared to starting the foreclosure from scratch. In the judicial states, final judgment of foreclosure is recorded to summarize the total amount due in the upset foreclosure sale. In the non-judicial states, prior to the foreclosure sale, a notice of trustee's sale is recorded as one of the documents. At the end of the foreclosure case, a sheriff's deed (in judicial states) or a trustee's deed (in non-judicial states) is filed to transfer the right to the property to a new owner.

Most states follow this sequence of document filings, but there are exceptions. In Maryland, for example, the civil court docket of the foreclosure case would reflect the depth of the case. In New York, the lis pendens is filed in the civil courts (as opposed to the county records) and the case docket for the foreclosure case would be used to determine the depth of the case. It's always beneficial to know that a foreclosure case is almost over, and the property is scheduled for the foreclosure sale (sheriff's sale or trustee's sale), making the note investment more attractive, as the intended exit strategy is almost completed. There are many more real estate title documents that give the investor hints as to the depth of the foreclosure process but, for the sake of simplicity, these common document types are enough for the beginning investor.

In all cases, once the foreclosure sale occurs, the foreclosure deed is recorded in the county records to show the transfer of ownership. In the case of foreclosure deed cancellation with a foreclosure deed recorded in error, there is a document (rescission of foreclosure deed) to void the property transfer. In fact, the rescission documents are frequently used to void any previously recorded documents.

## Servicing of Lien Holders

I cannot stress enough the importance of proper procedure in foreclosure servicing. Before the foreclosure action is started, the attorney filing the foreclosure must notify all property interest holders of the foreclosure action to allow them to bid on the property at the foreclosure sale. If the attorney does not properly notify one of the parties, the foreclosure may be undone, and the same expense may be required to refile it, delaying your opportunity to monetize your investment.

## Standing in Court

Equally important in the foreclosure process is to make sure the chain of assignments of mortgage does not have any breaks (disconnects), and that the foreclosing party that is filing the foreclosure case is the last assignee of record in the county recorder's office. When the assignment to the foreclosing party is not recorded, or the assignment chain has a break, the investor must spend additional time and money to resolve this issue by filing the appropriate documents. Some examples include a gap assignment, lost assignment affidavit, corrective assignment of mortgage and rescission of assignment. We'll go deeper into assignment breaks in later chapters.

# Continuing a Started Foreclosure Case

Buying a mortgage note in the middle of the foreclosure action may not be an issue for the investor. The foreclosing party who is also the seller may assign the rights to the investor, who is also the buyer, at any stage of the foreclosure case, as a plaintiff party assignment. In fact, even after the foreclosure is final, there is a document called *assignment of bid* that would assign the rights to the property from the seller of the note to the buyer of the note.

# The Foreclosure Collateral Package

Technically speaking, the foreclosing party must possess a true and original note (signed by the borrower in blue ink) to start the foreclosure. This is an important item to have on your checklist before a note purchase. The custodian (the company that holds the original note in a fireproof safe) should have possession of the original note. The copy of the original note should be in the collateral package offered to you by the seller as proof that, after the purchase, the buyer will have the full legal right to foreclose on the property. The note investor must always verify that the original note copy is present. In the case it's not present, I suggest you request an image of the original note from the seller before the note sale is final.

# Closing Thoughts on Foreclosure

Foreclosure is a great exit strategy on your note investment, as it eliminates unsecured debts like credit card judgments, hospital liens, any junior position mortgages and any junior position liens. Therefore, when an investor flips the property after the foreclosure, those judgments and junior liens would not attach to the property. Liens that are considered senior over the mortgage would always survive the foreclosure and would attach to the property. These liens will need to be paid off to remove them from the title and create a free and clear property. Senior liens were discussed in the prior chapter.

As a refresher, real estate taxes, HOA liens, some mechanics liens and any city/municipal/county/utility liens would be considered senior position liens over the first position mortgage. Your title due diligence process should be designed to reveal the relationship of your subject mortgage (the mortgage you're interested in buying) to other liens on the property. At the same time, you need to determine which liens will survive the foreclosure action and which liens would have to be paid off.

Before I guide you through designing your perfect due diligence workflow, let's review all the common exit strategies.

# CHAPTER FOURTEEN

# EXIT STRATEGIES FOR NOTE INVESTORS: DEED IN LIEU

One of the less popular exit strategies for the note investor is the deed in lieu of foreclosure (frequently called "DIL"). In essence, the borrower gives up the property to the lender; in return, the lender forgives the remaining debt on the mortgage. Sometimes this is called the "cash for keys" exit strategy. The benefit to the borrower is that his or her credit history is not impacted as much as they would be by the foreclosure action, because the lender/investor typically pays any relocation expenses to move the borrower from the property. Also, there is no chance for a deficiency judgment from the lender against the borrower, as opposed to the foreclosure case which does not result in the appropriate compensation to the lender.

*A Note of Warning:* In deeds in lieu of foreclosure, any and all judgments against the borrower or property will attach to the property, if not previously released or cured. Typically, only free and clear properties are considered for deed in lieu.

## Deed in Lieu Documents and Process

A deed in lieu of foreclosure document is typically recorded together with an estoppel affidavit in the county records and signed by the borrower to transfer the ownership to the last assignee of record. Again, the importance of a clean chain of assignment is key to the proper execution of the deed in lieu.

In most of cases, the DIL is drafted by an attorney licensed in the state where the property is located while the title company issues a title policy to protect the lender in case of unforeseen liens or lien holders. In today's market, executing the DIL with a cooperating borrower is a simple process. Typically, mobile notaries travel to the borrower's home to sign and witness the DIL documents and notarize the execution. I would not be surprised if, in the near future, DIL preparation and execution will be performed online using signature and figure printing. For all the entrepreneurs reading this book, online signature and figure print technology is the future for borrower signing.

If the borrower went through bankruptcy and all the unsecured judgments are released, the investor in the first position lien would have yet another exit strategy option – deed in lieu of foreclosure or short-sale – without worrying that the junior judgments will attach to the property.

Before we jump into title due diligence, let's cover a few note investing alternatives.

# CHAPTER FIFTEEN

# ALTERNATIVE INVESTMENT STRATEGIES: CONTRACT FOR DEED

One of the more popular unconventional options for investors has become an investment into contracts for deed (also called "rent-to-own"). Contracts for deed are similar to mortgages in terms of enforcement; however, the owner of the property is a lender (or investor), and the borrower is a tenant in the property until the contract is fully paid. The lender has more rights to the property and can shorten the cycle of tenant removal instead of going through a full-blown owner-occupied foreclosure. Some investors sell off the partial contract for deed (a percentage of the contract) to spread the risk of investing between multiple investors. The entry point for investors is typically very low, which makes this an attractive alternative for beginners.

From the title perspective, the contract for deed may or may not be recorded in the county records. If recorded, it should appear as an open mortgage or contract against the property, and the property owner should still be the lender until the contract matures (all payments are made per contract obligation). The judgments against the tenant (borrower) will never attach to the real estate property until the contract for deed matures and the deed for the borrower is executed.

## Documents and Assignments

The contract for deed is equivalent to a mortgage, but the assignment of contract for deed from seller to buyer is represented by a deed of ownership, and not by an assignment of mortgage. Since the owner of the property is a lender, the deed transfers the rights to collect on the contract from the old owner to the new deed owner.

The contract for deed is one of the primary investment choices for a number of hedge funds. One of the major players in the contract for deed market is Colonial Funding, managed by my very good friends, Eddie Speed and Bob Repass. If you are an investor entering the market for contracts for deed, I would certainly recommend contacting them for guidance and advice.

# CHAPTER SIXTEEN

# CHAIN OF ASSIGNMENT BREAKS AND HOW TO FIX THEM

## Let's Begin with the Basics

The assignment chain represents all the assignments of mortgage documents related to the same mortgage and connected by the parties involved. The assignment chain also refers to the subject mortgage in the body of the assignment document. The assignment of mortgage is related to a mortgage only if there is a valid reference of mortgage mentioned on the assignment document, as well as a valid description of the mortgage, the signature of the prior interest holder and a notary stamp. Typically, there are two parties involved in the mortgage sale or transaction: the assignor (the seller) and the assignee (the buyer).

The assignments are reviewed in chronological order, from the oldest to the newest, and this is usually the way assignments are represented on the title search abstract. A break in the assignment chain – a term used by the title and mortgage community – is when the assignee of the prior assignment does not match the assignor on the next assignment. In cases of assignee mergers, acquisitions or name changes on the prior assignment document, the assignor on the next assignment document should mention the prior assignor's name, and who the loan was acquired by, along with language clearly showing the transition of companies. For example, if the assignee of the prior assignment was Countrywide Home Loan Servicing LP, the assignor on the assignment executed in 2015 would read as Bank of America NA f/k/a BAC Home Loan Servicing LP f/k/a Countrywide Home Loan Servicing LP.

# The Importance of Assignment Breaks

Why are breaks in the assignment chain important? The last assignment of record for a given mortgage provides the standing in court for the last assignee to file a foreclosure action or collect on the mortgage. If there's a break in the assignment chain of the mortgage, the borrower may challenge the standing of the last assignee in the chain, arguing that the chain of the assignment is broken (or not connected), so the last assignee of record does not have the right to file for foreclosure. Until the chain of assignment is fixed, this agreement could lead to a dismissal of the foreclosure action. If the chain of assignment is not fixed, the mortgage assignment chain might show that a different party is the rightful owner of the note (prior assignee) with rights to foreclose. To avoid this, there are a number of ways to fix the assignment break.

# Ways to Fix the Break in the Chain

1. **Lost Assignment Affidavit or Gap Assignment:** When the assignment is missing from the assignment chain that connects the assignee from the prior assignment to the assignor on the next assignment, a lost assignment affidavit or gap assignment may be filed to "patch" the assignment gap. The lost assignment affidavit is signed by a prior assignee in the chain to certify that the assignment was, indeed, never filed and not recorded in the county records, although the intent was to record the assignment at the time of the mortgage transfer.

2. **Corrective Assignment:** In case of erroneous assignment – where the assignee was incorrectly mentioned, the subject mortgage reference was invalid, or there are signature, notary or legal issues present on the recorded assignment – the corrective assignment of mortgage or re-recorded assignment of mortgage is executed and filed in the county.

**3. Rescission of Assignment:** If the assignment is filed in error or prematurely, the rescission of assignment of mortgage is filed to void or nullify the assignment.

There are many other things to consider in order to have a clean assignment chain for a mortgage. Assignments in and out of MERS should also be consistent and accurate, and mention the correct MIN number as a part of the assignment document. The signor for MERS should be an official signor registered with MERS. If the signor of the assignment signs as an attorney for the lender, the power of attorney reference should be mentioned as part of the assignment document recorded in the county records.

Mis-indexed or mis-recorded assignments can also show up in the county registry. These are cases where the assignment document is actually recorded, and the chain of assignment has no breaks, but the recorder indexed the document with the wrong property, wrong legal description, misspelled borrower's name or different mortgage reference. These mis-indexing cases happen in a small percentage of loans, but they do happen on a regular basis. There is no need to re-file the document; resolving this issue is as easy as sending an e-mail to the recorder with the document number in question and correction details.

In some counties, the recorder system is only able to index the documents by the parties involved, making it difficult to find the assignments in these counties (indexed by assignor and assignee). For example, if the assignment is indexed by assignor Bank of America and assignee Wells Fargo Bank, it may generate a hundred thousand results for assignment documents matching the assignor or assignee's name, meaning you have to look for the proverbial needle in the haystack.

If the seller of the asset had possession of the note in the assignment chain, the assignment into the seller must be executed to show the note transfer. If the assignment into seller is not recorded in the county records, this may be considered a break in the chain.

# Due Diligence Advice

When purchasing a large portfolio of assets, it's important to verify that the last assignee of record for all assets matches the seller and, in the cases where the seller does not show on record through the assignment, you have to examine the collateral for the asset to verify that the copy of the unrecorded subject mortgage assignment into seller is available. There may be an unrecorded assignment image that can verify the seller's standing and fix the chain. Additionally, if the title company reports a gap or break in the assignment chain, you need to determine whether the collateral image file may contain the recorded assignment document that patches the chain of assignment. In this case, the missing assignment in the chain may have simply been mis-indexed or mis-recorded.

# CHAPTER SEVENTEEN

## VESTING AND ORIGINATION DEFECT RISK GRADING

In this chapter, we start putting the learned concepts together and covering some common due diligence issues. This is where we begin to evaluate data from our title research and assign an investment risk factor to different issues and events. By grouping issues into categories, we are able to analyze complex portfolios with risk-level methodology based on facts. Let's start with vesting issues and get into defect risk grouping.

## **Defining Vesting Defect**

A vesting defect on a title is when you see that the borrower on the subject mortgage is different from the current vested owner of the property. This ownership incongruity may be very severe to the mortgage notes investor or it may be a non-issue. Severe vesting issues for note investors reflect a past event that eliminated the secured interest of the mortgage from the property, while non-issue defects are events that do not change the mortgage attachment to the property or the enforceability of the mortgage.

The title search report (an O&E report, in this case) would be an ideal tool to discover these defects. This is exactly why title search plays a major role during the due diligence process.

In the real estate investor's world, vesting defects relate to the recovery of the mortgage enforceability by curing the vesting issues defects, if required. Obviously, there are curable and non-curable vesting defects. Non-curable (AKA severe) defects, by definition, are ownership transfer events in the chain of title when the ownership is transferred to a new party, eliminating all interests of the lender from the property.

# Vesting Defects: Some Examples

In many states, tax deeds (even unrecorded tax deeds with tax deed applications in progress) or municipal deeds are considered unrecoverable change-of-ownership events. An HOA foreclosure deed would wipe off the mortgage in Nevada, while an HOA deed in Florida is still subject to the first position mortgage and does not eliminate the mortgage attachment from title or property. Depending on each state's HOA deed legal statute, the mortgage may or may not attach to the property after an HOA foreclosure. (For a refresher on state statutes for HOA super lien states, go back to the HOA Lien section.)

Subject mortgage foreclosure is a common vesting defect. While the distressed mortgage with an active foreclosure is scheduled to be sold to the note investor as a part of a portfolio trade, the mortgage may be foreclosed before the trade is settled. In my experience, only a small percentage of loans in large portfolios where the subject mortgage went through a foreclosure (with a foreclosure deed recorded) are no longer considered a note. Typically, foreclosed loans (REOs) are kicked back to the seller at the due diligence phase of the note purchase, since REO properties are not part of the seller reps and warrants. The problem in keeping the REO properties part of the loan portfolio sale is unpredictability, as well as a lack of control over sold properties on a foreclosure auction or sheriff's sale to a third party.

The same issue arises when the lender has executed a deed in lieu of foreclosure on the subject mortgage with the borrower. The investor has no control of the timing for future sales of the properties to third parties during the deed in lieu ownership change.

When note investors evaluate a portfolio of loans, each asset with a vesting issue (typically, the borrower name not matching the vested owner's name) can be placed in one of four groups, each associated with a certain level of risk (more detail later in this chapter):

## Group 1: The Severe Defect Group

A severe vesting defect is one where there is no recourse, rescission or redemption. Tax deeds in non-redeemable states would be a severe defect for the note investor, because the lender loses all interest in the property. A prior lien or mortgage foreclosure (making the prior lien senior to the mortgage) is another example where the senior position allows foreclosure ahead of the subject mortgage. A prior lien or prior mortgage foreclosure, however, might be covered for losses by a lender's title policy, but it can take a long time to receive the compensation from the title insurance underwriter. In my opinion, if this defect is discovered during the title due diligence, and before the final closing date on the asset pool or a note, it should be kicked back to the seller.

Previously, we discussed a subject mortgage foreclosure and a deed in lieu of ownership change. Let's say that our subject mortgage being released or satisfied in the public records would create a severe defect; the note or mortgage is no longer attached to the property. In this common case, the property was sold to a third party before the sale of the note was final, or when the borrower refinanced.

Another issue covered previously involves an HOA foreclosure deed in the states of Nevada and Massachusetts. In these non-redeemable ownership transfers (based on current case law), all mortgages are wiped off the property.

If the borrower is not found on the chain of title – meaning his or her name was never recorded – this is also a severe defect. This is rare, but can happen when the deed is rejected by the recorder during the filing of the document for whatever reason, and the corrected deed was never filed. From the title perspective, this is called a "wild" mortgage, where the mortgage is recorded against an owner who is not showing up in the chain of title. A similar situation is when the vesting deed is mis-indexed, meaning the recorder indexed the document by a different name or legal entity, making it impossible for title companies to find the deed. Luckily, this defect is not as severe, as it can be cured by requesting that the recorder correct the current indexing.

Finally, severe vesting issues arise during the origination of a mortgage – mostly related to signature problems or notarization issues. For example, if a property is owned by a husband and wife, but only the wife signs the mortgage, the lender has no right to remove the husband from the property in the foreclosure action. Similar problems occur when a wife signs a power of attorney document for both herself and her husband, or a mortgage is missing notary stamps. Either case could create a severe issue for the enforceability of the mortgage.

## Group 2: The Unresolved Defect Group

Unresolved vesting issues occur when the transfer of ownership is completed as it relates to the first position mortgage, but introduces a cloud on the title's ownership. Unresolved defects – in this case, recovering the clear enforceability of a first position lien – typically cost investors a lot of money and time. For that reason, assets with unresolved vesting issues are typically traded at a deep discount.

One of the common unresolved vesting issues is a subordinate HOA lien foreclosure (but not in Nevada or Massachusetts) subject to the first position mortgage. When an HOA foreclosure is final and the HOA foreclosure deed is recorded, the vesting becomes clouded until the lender negotiates the cancellation of the HOA foreclosure deed from public records, and settles on an amount of money. If the third-party investor buys the property at the HOA foreclosure sale, the first position lender typically forecloses on the property to resolve the ownership, then goes through a title action in federal court. In Florida, it's common to see separate foreclosures on the same property at the same time, one by the lender and another by the HOA. For situations where the HOA foreclosure deed and mortgage foreclosure deed (called certificate of title in Florida) are filed one after another, the cloud on the title is resolved by a rescission of one of the deeds, typically the HOA deed. I will have more on this scenario a bit later.

The second position mortgage holder can foreclose on the property out of position, however, for the purposes of renting the property, collecting rent and battling the first lien in court, once the first lien starts the foreclosure. There may be a number of reasons why the second position mortgage holder (also called the second lienholder) can file a foreclosure action and record the foreclosure deed first, well before the first position mortgage foreclosure deed, yet while still subject to the senior lien(s). The goal for the second lienholder to foreclose quickly on the property is to make sure there's enough time to rent the property out (and collect some revenue) before the first lien foreclosure becomes final. I have heard of cases where the second lien holder was collecting rent for over two years before the first lien foreclosed.

If the borrower files for Chapter 7 or Chapter 11 bankruptcy, and the first position mortgage holder is not well represented in the bankruptcy court, the bankruptcy-appointed trustee may transfer the property to a liquidation trust or a third party unassociated with the chain of title. This action is to satisfy the bankruptcy debt, and is known as a bankruptcy trustee transfer vesting issue. Additionally, the borrower's attorney can carefully draft the bankruptcy plan with verbiage to strike the first lien from the title. If a bankruptcy judge approved the plan, the first lien may be considered released. (If you need a refresher on this topic, go back to the bankruptcy chapter.)

In very rural parts of the country, the county assessors assign individual parcel numbers to large chunks of the land. In these areas, owners are able to sell off parts of their land to a new owner, frequently registered under the same parcel number. In some cases, these large or unusual parcel splits can present an unresolved defect. This type of sale must be done with the lender's approval, in which case the lender would file a document called a partial release of mortgage to release the parcel of land free and clear. After these land sales, it's important to keep track of the new legal description for any future documents recorded in the county to make sure they describe the land in the subject mortgage as an original legal description, to help prevent an accidental foreclosure on the new parcel owner's property.

If the legal description of the foreclosed property is wrong, the judge will dismiss any foreclosure case and require you to refile with the corrected legal description, only after the foreclosure corrective documents are recorded. Unfortunately, this is a common error in the public records. In some cases, the owner may sell parts of his or her land subject to "open mortgage." This means both owners of the split parcel would need to be served during any court actions. In more complex cases, easements, oil and gas rights, and rights of way affecting the subject parcel must be accurately reflected in the legal documents. If an error is made in the legal description of oil and gas rights, the new owners will find themselves in the courtroom fighting or surrendering rights to something they never owned in the first place.

### Group 3: The Informational Defects Group

There are many vesting issues that may be treated as informational, but we will only cover the most common cases seen on title reports.

**Estate Transfers Due to Borrower Death** – When the borrower dies and the ownership was solely in the borrower's name, the estate case is opened to determine the heirs of the estate. The subject mortgage would still attach to the property and the estate of the borrower. In the case of foreclosure, however, the court documents must be drafted carefully to make sure that not only the estate of the borrower is named in the proceedings, but also any and all heirs and assigns. Once the estate is closed and heirs are disclosed, they must be included in all future proceedings. The estate may have the right to liquidate the assets, including the property, subject to all liens and judgments against the deceased, and the new owner will still be liable to the subject mortgage, even though the ownership will be different.

**Transfers to a Third Party (Private Individuals, Corporations, LLCs, etc.)** – Often, because of a transfer of ownership from the original borrower to a third party, limited liability corporation or trust, the owner of the property does not match the borrower. In these cases, the subject mortgage will still attach to the property and the new owner will be liable for paying it off. The only twist to the ownership change from the lender's side is that they must make sure that the new owner is named in the foreclosure court proceedings, as well as any and all judgment and lien holders from the time of the mortgage origination to the present. I have seen a case where the LLC became a new owner of a property with the US Department of Justice lien recorded against the LLC, and not the original borrower (the borrower was the owner of the LLC). The title company who ran the title due diligence (an off-shore firm) did not run the LLC company for liens and judgments, foreclosing on the property without serving the Department of Justice, only discovering during the resale that the US DoJ lien must be paid off to receive a partial release of the lien to sell the property free and clear. The error of not running the LLC (and of using an off-shore title company) cost the investor almost $40,000.

**Property is a Unit in a Cooperative Building/Complex** – From the document perspective, mortgages taken out for co-ops must be treated completely differently from the mortgages against a typical residential real estate property. Co-ops are very popular in New York and New Jersey, and rarely encountered in other parts of the country. In these cases, the entire condo building is owned by a cooperative association, while the unit owner owns a small percent of the common property through a proprietary lease. The mortgage document is never recorded as a mortgage in the county records; the only recorded document in the county records is a UCC (uniform commercial code) document, which mentions the borrower's name, the lender's name and the legal description of the property. The note is executed the same way as any standard real estate transaction, but the assignment of mortgage will be executed and recorded differently as a UCC assignment document at the county office. In some cases (making the co-op research more complex), when the owner is a corporation or LLC, the UCC documents may be also recorded with the secretary of state, either where the property is located (for individuals) or where the corporation is incorporated (for corporations). The accurate representation of the borrower as a company's incorporation should help title companies track the UCC documents, by searching the state of incorporation. The title report will look different from the standard deed and mortgage chain perspective; on the title report, the owner of the property will be shown as a co-op association, while the subject mortgage will be reported as a UCC, with assignments as UCC assignments and amendments. If the UCC is correctly recorded in the county records, the mortgage attaches to the property without any issues.

**Parcel Splits of Small Land Area (i.e., Deeding Easements or Rights of Way)** – We've already touched on splits of land in rural areas. Let's discuss small parcel splits, or sell-off deeds, to the municipality, utility company or third party. As before, the investor must pay attention to an adjusted parcel legal description from the subject mortgage. The new legal description might be affected by re-assignment of parcel numbers, 911 address changes or revisions to the plat map. All these minor changes should also be tracked and referenced in updated legal descriptions in all mortgage-related documents recorded after the event of the change took place.

Let's say Verizon installed a FIOS access panel on a property, for example, and executed an easement agreement with the owner for the right to use the land for their installation. The easement was also allowed by the lender, but in all future mortgage-related documents, the adjusted legal description for the subject property must reflect this easement, otherwise Verizon would file a title claim against the new owners after a foreclosure or property transfer, saying the easement was illegally foreclosed upon.

**Subject Mortgage Foreclosure with Subsequent Rescission/Vacation of FC** – Sometimes the title search will have a rescission of the foreclosure deed, meaning a cancellation of the deed. In these cases, the last grantee of record may be shown as a lender or investor buying a property at the auction, with the cancellation or rescission of the transfer shown in the documents. Once the rescission is recorded, the subject mortgage will reattach to the property.

## Group 4: The Non-Issue Group

Sometimes the difference between the borrower's name and the owner's name contributes to the quitclaim or in-family transfer. Here are a few common cases of these non-issue defects.

**Inter-Family Deed Transfers** – Whenever a husband and wife have different last names, or there is an in-family (gift) transfer between relatives at zero ($0) value, the subject mortgage still attaches to the property, even though the owner's name and borrower's name don't match.

**Standard Transfers into Land Trusts** – A very common transfer in the states of California, Nevada, Illinois and Washington is a property transfer into the family or land trust. Again, while the name of the owner and borrower do not match, the subject mortgage would still attach to the property.

**Marital Name Changes** – A common vesting non-issue defect is a name change, commonly due to a marriage.

**Non-Material Deed Matters (Adding Additional Owners, Adding Survivor/Heir Interest, etc.)** – A common vesting mismatch is caused by the addition and/or removal of family members to the ownership or heir ownership transfer after the estate settles. Like the others in this group, these are non-issues when it comes to the enforcement of the mortgage.

# CHAPTER EIGHTEEN

## BUILDING A DUE DILIGENCE PLATFORM

If you understand the material covered to this point, it's time to start building your due diligence platform to invest in real estate assets. You're already aware of some of the basic factors that can hurt you, and you know how to find the issues by looking at title reports. Yes, there are many more legal aspects and quirky local regulations that can affect your bottom line, but you know enough to get started. So here we go.

I am extremely proud that, within the portfolio analysis workflow developed by ProTitleUSA, we integrated a great deal of legal and title complexities. We even created a new product which we offer free to our corporate clients (bulk asset buyers) – the title and tax dashboard with limited title exam. We have also designed a workflow where we learn from local jurisdiction regulations and integrate additional steps or checks. It's not quite artificial intelligence (AI), but it is based on a human learning engine that benefits from experiences and information accumulated over the course of ten years.

## Evolution of Due Diligence

For many investors, our title and tax dashboard is a completely unknown and refreshing product. For years, the title industry was dominated by a few title companies delivering title searches or O&Es without providing the additional information investors needed to help them make proper investment decisions. In fact, many investors built their own staff to process (read page-by-page) O&E reports and enter asset opinions into proprietary systems or spreadsheets. This title exam and data entry process would take weeks, on top of the usual delivery of O&E reports by vendors. There was always a chance of human error in carrying over the information from reports, analysis and title exam. The timeline to deliver all aspects of the due diligence on the portfolios of assets – including O&E reports, data entry, title exam and analysis – would be measured in months. To make matters worse (take more time and increase chances for error), the information from the title search (sometimes called title meta data) would not be reused for future investor needs, such as document preparation and recording or boarding loans with a servicer.

## ProTitleUSA Approach (use as Template)

ProTitleUSA solved most of these time-consuming tasks, but not all, leaving a much smaller due diligence effort for the investor or third party. The Note Pool Due Diligence Flowchart on page 102 is a diagram I built to better explain the benefits of our system. The goal of the workflow is to create a robust system of verification for all assets in the portfolio – automatically – raising the "failed" flag only for the assets that did not pass our predefined test criteria. The assets that failed the title exam or dashboard checks would be marked for further review, so they could be examined by the investor to understand why the flags were raised.

The overall goal of the workflow is to reduce the number of human reviews of asset fails to a minimum. As an example, in a portfolio of 1,000 assets, it might only be necessary to review the 50 assets that had a "failed" flag raised for one reason or another. Failed flags can be any of the items we discussed earlier in the book – vesting issues with the borrower not having the same name as the current owner, subject mortgage not being in the first position, superior lien or judgment appears to be ahead of the mortgage, etc. In addition to sorting through the liens and judgments that would survive the foreclosure, or can knock foreclosure out of position, it's also important to sort the liens by recording date, comparing those to the subject mortgage recording date. In essence, the subject mortgage recording date becomes the sorting criterion for each lien on each reviewed asset.

When buying a note, it's important to verify that the title policy (TP or TPOL) is a part of the asset collateral produced for your review by the seller. This represents title insurance to a lender or any assigned parties (you, the buyer) to protect against any claims made by third parties as a result of a judgment, lien or mortgage recorded prior to subject mortgage origination date. This would suggest that, if there was a superior lien prior to the origination date of the mortgage, the title policy would cover any losses due to the prior lien. Conversely, if the lien is placed after the origination date of the mortgage, it will take priority based on the lien type and federal or state law.

## Hints for Building Your Due Diligence System

When building a due diligence system from scratch, you are going to be using a basic comparison of the asset-level data with a predetermined set of data checks to make an asset pass or fail. We call the process an automated title exam. The title exam parameters (the data you compare assets against) can be static or dynamic with respect to the asset or property. Static parameters are based on the state law or statute of limitation; for example, in Louisiana, the tax deed redemption is three years (a static value). Dynamic parameters are property-specific, meaning each individual lien or issue with the chain of title is unique to the title search. The ProTitleUSA workflow combines static and dynamic parameters into a single title and tax dashboard for a quicker review of the portfolio.

## Putting It All Together

There are typically three parallel workflows for title due diligence:

1. Tax and title issues review
2. Enforceability of the mortgage with assignment break checking
3. Asset collateral review with cross-referencing of the title and tax dashboard results

In the diagram below, the parallel workflow is displayed as white boxes across the bottom. The box outlined in red represents the typical deliverable of a ProTitleUSA title and tax due diligence report. Each workflow should result in the cross-verification of asset-level data delivered by the title research company via a title search report and title and tax dashboard, instead of relying solely on collateral delivered by the seller. Let's discuss each due diligence flow in detail.

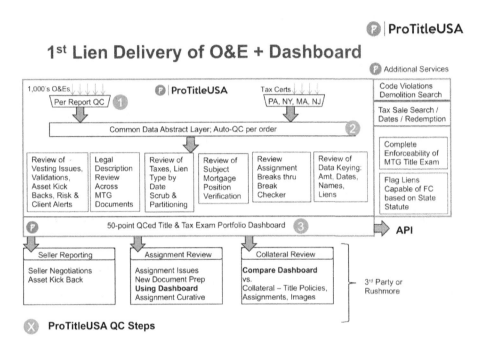

## Workflow 1: Tax and Title Issues Review

The first sub-workflow in the due diligence cycle (bottom left box in the diagram) is final tax and title review. This process relies heavily on the accuracy of the title and tax dashboard after reviewing all failed flags raised by the title search company. Each failed flag should be associated with a risk grade for buying the asset. The calculated risk of ownership for any failed asset should also include the costs of curing the asset from any and all identified title defects.

Lost or unrecoverable assets (failed assets with severe defects) should be kicked back to the seller or exchanged for an equivalent asset. Assets that fail with undetermined defects or liens (that could foreclose out of position) should be graded by the amount of money and time the investor would need to spend to cure the defect. For example, the cost to negotiate and file the release of an HOA lien can range anywhere from $500 to $1,000 and could take one to three months – and that's on top of the HOA lien negotiated pay-off.

The lien amount on the title and tax dashboard should also account for interest and penalties. Typically, the maximum allowable interest rate per state is used to estimate the current payoff from the lien principal amount. Once the risk grading is done, remaining assets can be marked for an initial exit strategy queue based on risk level, time to cure, amount of money needed to cure the defects or number of junior judgments against the borrower/owner or property. This information can be critical to project an ROI for each individual portfolio.

### *Workflow 2: Enforceability with Assignment Break Checking*

The second sub-workflow in the due diligence cycle (bottom middle box) has to do with assignment break checking and verifying enforceability of the mortgage. Ideally, the subject mortgage has no assignment chain breaks and the final assignment in the chain is the seller as the assignee. This is not always the case; maybe the county clerk recorded an assignment incorrectly, maybe the recorder indexed the assignment only by the lender's name, or maybe there's a legitimate assignment break and the investor or seller are responsible for filing missing assignments to resolve the break. Whatever the reason, the purpose of the second sub-workflow is to verify that the chain of assignments is indeed broken, or if there is simply an issue with the way the recorder indexed the document (in which case, the title search company can find it searching by legal, address, parcel number or borrower's name).

If the title search company flags a break in the assignment chain, every effort should be made to review the collateral for recorded images of the assignments for each asset, cross-verifying against the breaks found in the title search. In addition, the investor must approach these breaks keeping in mind the enforceability of the mortgage, always assuming the mortgage will end up in foreclosure court. In the borrower-contested foreclosure, the chain of assignment is the first thing reviewed by a judge and borrower's counsel to challenge the standing in court (for right to bring the foreclosure action). If the chain of assignment is broken, this is evidence that the investor does not hold the right to foreclose, meaning the foreclosure case may be dismissed until any assignment breaks are cured. In fact, if the assignment break is cured after a case is dismissed, the borrower can contest that, as well, so the investor and seller of the mortgage must have a plan to cure any breaks in the assignment chain before the note purchase is finalized. In my experience, each curative action on the assignment chain increases the risk of mortgage non-enforceability, as well as the expense of curing the defect (document preparation, recording fees, shipping and handling and, of course, the investor's time).

## *Workflow 3: Asset Collateral Review*

The third sub-workflow in the due diligence cycle (bottom right box) has to do with running the exception reports on the portfolio collateral and verifying all items that would need to be re-verified by the title search company. For example, an O&E report picked up a prior unreleased mortgage, so it would be necessary to re-verify that the release was, indeed, recorded using additional information from the release document found in the collateral. In another example, the collateral images show the subject mortgage had a modification agreement executed, but the O&E report did not report any modifications. The title search company can use the sign date of the modification agreement to re-verify that the agreement was never recorded (a common occurrence, by the way).

# Covering All the Bases on Due Diligence

## *Water and Sewer*

Some investors choose to integrate a more comprehensive due diligence workflow outside of the standard three workflows discussed. Remember our discussion on all the liens and balances that would survive a foreclosure? In some states, water and sewer unpaid balances would attach to the property. If your primary exit strategy is foreclosure, water and sewer (utility) balance information can be a very valuable data point. In many states, if there are any outstanding water and sewer balances on the subject property, a foreclosure deed (or sheriff's deed) will be rejected by the recorder's office. This information is extremely tough to get since, during the due diligence, we must identify the utility company for a given property. In addition, not every utility company will surrender the information on the balance without a letter of representation. Typically, the seller of notes will issue a letter of representation (or letter of authority) to help the due diligence firm gain that information. Adding to the difficulty, if the water or sewer service is provided by a local government office, the response time may be extremely slow.

## *Bankruptcy*

Bankruptcy scrubs may be extremely useful to the investor and may reveal new exit strategies not considered previously. It may also be important to find out which liens or judgments became unsecured following a bankruptcy proceeding and are no longer attached to the property. To verify which judgments or liens have been stripped from the property, one would need to review the bankruptcy proceedings plan, as well as the bankruptcy discharge documents.

## *Code Violations, Permit Violations and Demolition*

On particularly "messy" assets (full of municipal liens), code violations, permit violations and demolition search should always be done (in my opinion). An O&E report will not show you if the property was scheduled for demolition due to city violations, as the demolition list is kept at the township or city where the property is located. In fact, a separate search must be conducted to review city or township records.

## Tax Sale and Redemption

The last due diligence search to mention – a very important one – is the tax sale and redemption search. When it comes to tax reporting, you need to understand exactly what an O&E report will provide, and what it won't. You will see the total delinquent amount of taxes for the property, as well as the real estate taxes amount due for the current year. But an O&E will not show if the property is scheduled for a tax sale or any of the important related information – the date of the tax sale, the full or partial amount needed to cancel the tax sale, the last date to redeem, the redeeming instructions or the contacts. If you know that the taxes are delinquent on the property for multiple years, I would recommend ordering this search. This tax sale and redemption service may be an add-on to the O&E reports, with the dashboard reflecting only the subset of assets in danger of the tax sale, or the expiration of the redeemable tax deed. In other words, the investor may search only on the assets in danger of being lost to tax sale.

# CHAPTER NINETEEN

## BUILDING A DUE DILIGENCE PLATFORM: SECOND POSITION NOTE BUYERS

One of the most price-sensitive markets in the note business is the second position performing and non-performing note trading market. Typically, O&E reports cost too much for the purposes of the second lien investor; the margins are very slim. Second lien note investors count on the first position investors to pay any delinquent taxes on the subject property and clear any liens that would supersede the first position mortgage and the second position mortgage by default. The price of the second position mortgage varies, depending on whether the second position mortgage is secured by real estate property or unsecured from the real estate by foreclosure of the first position lien (or tax sale, bankruptcy or HOA deed, in some states). Additionally, the price of the second lien is also dependent on knowing if the first position lien is or isn't in active foreclosure, making the second position lien unsecured in the near future. At ProTitleUSA, we came up with a waterfall approach that would minimize the money spent for the due diligence, based on the results of each stage of the waterfall scheme. See on next page:

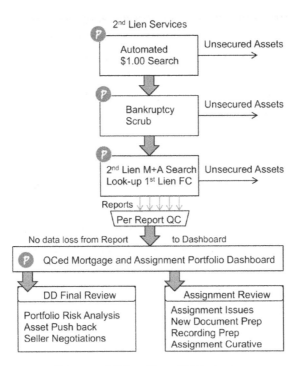

## First Stage of Second Lien Due Diligence

For the first stage of the due diligence on second position notes, there is a quick and easy way to sort out the unsecured second position liens. Typically, this is done pre-bid on the large pool of second position notes. I came up with the $1.00 per asset search. The idea behind this product is to create automation around validation of the ownership and last sale information, based on the nationwide assessor's records. I developed and implemented a method of comparing the second lien data points – such as mortgage amount, date of origination and borrower name – while our automation process scours data from the assessor records. The $1.00 per asset due diligence assumes that the second lien will have a high chance of being unsecured if 1. the owner of the property is different from the borrower on the loan tape, and 2. the sale of the property occurred after the origination date of the mortgage for a price of $1,000 or more.

After a full year of measuring, our automation was close to 97%

accurate in catching unsecured loans. Additionally, if the new owner of the property is a lender, we would also assume that the first position foreclosure wiped off the second position lien, making it unsecured. If the owner is an HOA-based company, it implies that the HOA foreclosed on the property and, in states like Nevada, that would wipe off the mortgage.

Finally, if the owner is a treasurer or tax investor, this may hint that the property may be lost to tax sale and, therefore, the mortgage would be unsecured in the non-redeemable states (refer back to the tax section to review the redeemable and non-redeemable states). This search does not, however, include a bankruptcy search, which should be a part of the workflow to weed out the unsecured loans.

### Second Stage of Second Lien Due Diligence

The process described above would enable the second lien investor to narrow down the list of second liens that are unsecured. The next stage of the waterfall approach is a bankruptcy scrub. This stage can be automated, as well, to deliver useful results for due diligence analysis, including 1. determining if there was a bankruptcy case found for the borrower, and 2. if there was a bankruptcy case, determining if there were any orders to strike a lien, or an approved bankruptcy plan that involved removing the second position lien, making it unsecured. If there was no bankruptcy case found, this would imply that the second lien was not affected by the bankruptcy proceedings or court orders. If there was a bankruptcy match on the borrower's name, one would need to verify the bankruptcy case documents and docket for any orders that could impact the second position lien. This is the last automation stage in the waterfall due diligence for second lien investors.

### Third Stage of Second Lien Due Diligence

Finally, in-person (in-county) title search due diligence for second liens represents the most accurate view of the second position lien per the county records. However, I wanted this search – specific to second liens – to be half the price of the O&E report, which we managed to accomplish nationwide. At ProTitleUSA, the (long) name of this search is the "second position mortgage and assignment search with foreclosure check of the first position lien and check on chain." The goal behind this search is threefold:

1. Checking for any assignment breaks of the subject second lien, verifying the position to be second
2. Confirming the first position lien foreclosure status – not in active foreclosure, in active foreclosure or foreclosed
3. Verifying that the chain of title does not have any tax deed, court deed or HOA deed transfers (this is a search done by a searcher – not automation – so the results are expected to be 100% accurate)

After going through all three waterfall stages of second position lien due diligence, the investor may now accurately decide on pricing the investment. Some investors using ProTitleUSA choose to run the $1.00 per asset search pre-bid during the acquisition stage and the remaining stages once the pool is under contract. Some investors run the $1.00 search and bankruptcy scrubs at both the pre-bid and final stage (which is more expensive) once the pool is under contract.

A few of ProTitleUSA's second lien clients had properties where the subordination agreement was never filed, making the second position lien in first position, according to the recording date. To recover their position, the first position lien holder would have to negotiate with the second lien investor to file the subordination agreement, or file a title claim against the title company responsible for the error. For cases where the second position lien holder cannot contact the first position lien holder – if the original lender or title company went out of business, for example – the second position lien investor may choose to file a foreclosure on the property out of position, knowing that the error (no subordination agreement filed) put the second lien holder in first position related to the mortgage.

# CHAPTER TWENTY

# BUILDING A DUE DILIGENCE PLATFORM: COMMERCIAL NOTE BUYERS

Commercial properties are properties zoned as industrial, government, mixed use, agricultural or commercial by an assessor. Any mortgage secured by these properties is considered a commercial mortgage. Common types of commercial loans include multi-family/mixed, construction/builder loans, malls, hotels/motels, office buildings, gas stations/car washes, commercial land, railroads, commercial leaseholds, mobile parks, cell towers, churches, government buildings or government-owned land. Each of the common types introduces a standalone level of complexity during the due diligence.

Commercial asset title due diligence is typically handled before the bid, which is the opposite of residential due diligence. Therefore, the investor is committing a significant due diligence budget upfront without any assurance that the commercial asset will be won at the end of the process. There's a good reason for this upfront expense, though – the acquisition price of commercial assets is much higher than residential. In addition, any title issue may cost the investor a significant amount of money to cure, and the commercial in-county searches are much more expensive then residential (because of the additional research time and documents required to complete the search).

## *Due Diligence Complexity for Commercial Titles*

As a commercial note investor buying a mortgage, you're not just investing in the note, but also in rents and leases revenue and/or Uniform Commercial Code (UCC) collateral. In the case of a default, the commercial note investor can enforce the mortgage or any rents collected by the borrower or tools of the trade (described in the UCC document) as a part of the collateral of the commercial note at the time of the origination. For example, if a borrower is the owner of a strip mall who takes out a commercial mortgage on the mall and rents out individual units, upon default on the mortgage payments, the lender may claim the right of rent collection per a document called assignment of rents and leases. In another example, if a borrower buys a building and builds a pizza shop covered by the same commercial mortgage using the same money for a pizza oven, the UCC document would guarantee the lender's ownership in all non-real estate, non-rental items, including tools of the trade – in this case, the pizza oven.

As you can see from these examples, the investor must pay attention not only to assigning the commercial mortgage, but also to the assignment of rents and leases (yes, that is the official name of the document assigning the right to collect rents), as well as the UCC assignment. As a rule, as part of the transfer of a commercial note, three separate documents should be executed and recorded at the county of the property – assignment of mortgage, assignment of rents and leases, and UCC assignment. This way, all collateral is properly assigned under the commercial paper.

To make things more complicated, since 2002, all commercial lenders started filing UCC documents with the secretary of state in the state of incorporation of the borrowing entity, and not at the county. In other words, if you purchased a commercial property, the UCC may be filed at the secretary of state's office where the property is located, but if the buyer is a corporation or LLC incorporated in Delaware, the UCC will be filed at the Delaware secretary of state's office.

As you can see, if the title report and secretary of state search results in the discovery of a break of the assignment or UCC chain, curative actions may be required not just within the mortgage recorded documents, but with the UCC and assignment of rents and leases documents, as well. Additionally, the UCC documents must be continued every five years from the date of filing, otherwise they will lapse or expire without any chance of renewal. There are a few exceptions to this rule – utility financing statements and record of mortgage as financing statements (as an example, in the case of coops), and manufactured home affidavits expire after 30 years. Once the commercial mortgage gets released, the release of mortgage document, release of assignment of rents and leases document, and termination of the UCC document are filed at the filing place of the initial UCC.

The burdensome title examination of commercial loans doesn't end there. Not only must the corporation or LLC, as the owner, be checked for judgments, but each individual partner (or percentage owner) of the corporation must be checked, as well. In some cases, the structure of the corporation or LLC is not known from its public records. If you come across this situation, I recommend contacting the commercial mortgage/note seller to provide the disclosure of ownership, making sure your due diligence includes all owners and individuals.

Commercial mortgages have many types of documents that may have to be dealt with and/or assigned. Two of the common examples are the subordination and non-disturbance agreement (typically executed between the tenant and lender, which states that, in the case of any court action against the borrower, the tenant will not be disturbed) and the cross-collateral agreement (a document consolidating multiple debts into a single repayment agreement for the same lender). When the commercial property overlaps multiple counties, the mortgage and related documents must be recorded in each county belonging to the property.

### ProTitleUSA and the FDIC

During the banking financial crisis from 2008 to 2010, the FDIC selected ProTitleUSA as one of the primary vendors for commercial due diligence on all sales (auctions) for assets of the failed institutions the FDIC had to take over. Nine years later, we still run due diligence for the FDIC assets, both commercial and residential. Investors that purchased these assets were under an agreement with the FDIC to keep the assets on the books – without foreclosing – for a period of at least five years. Running updates on those loans years later revealed a lot of surprising issues. In many cases, especially with construction loans, careless investors lost parts (if not all) of the land lots covered under the original commercial mortgage to tax sales, municipal sales or foreclosures of mechanics liens. In the construction commercial space, investors must monitor any and all land splits or joins every 3-6 months. For example, if a condo builder took out a loan to build condos across a number of parcels, upon completion of the project, the assessor may have assigned new parcel numbers to each individual unit, according to the new plat map, subdivision or condo declaration. You need to watch for any changes in parcel numbers to make sure that taxes are being paid correctly, and that no mechanics liens pop up in the recorder's office which may become a superior lien over the commercial mortgage.

I am very proud to say that I have created a process within ProTitleUSA to simplify the commercial due diligence within our work flow and title exam, and to ensure that the information presented by ProTitleUSA on commercial deals is clear and accurate, and will help our clients make good investment decisions.

# Commercial Note Pool Due Diligence Flowchart

Additional Services

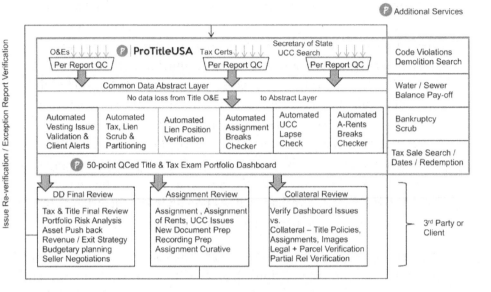

The three workflows described earlier for the residential note due diligence are also applicable to the commercial notes, except that commercial mortgages require additional checks. As a part of the title and tax commercial dashboard, you're not only checking for breaks in the chain of assignment of mortgages, but also in assignments of rents and leases. UCC documents must also be checked for assignments and renewals (continuations) within the required renew cycle. Judgments and liens must be further subdivided and categorized by judgments against the companies as borrowers versus judgments against the partners of the company or investors holding a percentage of corporate stock. In the flow diagram above, additional checks within the flow are highlighted in yellow. As a part of the automation and work flow process, ProTitleUSA has developed additional checks for UCC lapses and assignment of rents breaks.

# CHAPTER TWENTY-ONE

## COMMON ISSUES FOR REAL ESTATE OWNED BUYERS

Many ProTitleUSA clients like buying real estate properties at foreclosure auctions (sheriff's or trustee's sales); this is a very common investment. In fact, the biggest landlords in America are Wall Street firms like BlackRock and Black Stone. The attraction and popularity of buying property at a low auction price and renting or flipping it has made this market very competitive. However, not every investor knows about the common errors and pitfalls of this type of investment.

If you are buying properties at bank-owned auctions or in foreclosure, trustee's or sheriff's sales, the title search report is a must-have due diligence tool to verify whether the property is worth the investment. In fact, you – the investor – must understand which liens would survive the foreclosure and which liens would be wiped off the property. Too many people go with the popular notion that buying foreclosures will save them money, only to be very disappointed to find out they tied up their money for a long period of time and took a major loss due to outstanding liens. Using the title search to build an exit strategy for an REO investment is also the key to investment success.

## For Example

If there's an IRS lien against the borrower, flipping the property within 120 days is an ill-advised exit strategy. (Remember the 120-day IRS redemption period?) A title search will give you the information you need to make smarter decisions, including which interest holders were serviced and notified of the foreclosure sale. In some cases, even the plaintiff in a personal injury judgment against the borrower (and not the property) can demand a payoff to release their judgment from the property.

This actually happened to me. The lender foreclosed on the property and the property was about to be sold to a new owner. The attorney representing the buyer, while examining the servicing of the foreclosure sale, found a "slip and fall" judgment against the borrower that occurred on the sidewalk of a completely different property – and this plaintiff was never notified of the foreclosure sale. Once the attorney representing the buyer tried to get a release of all claims from the plaintiff (to release the subject property), the plaintiff demanded $10,000 to sign. This may not be fair or logical, but that is how the system works in America.

## REO-to-Rent Exit Strategy Issues

Another mostly unknown pitfall is the failure to look for rental restrictions as a part of the declaration of condominiums and by-laws. In some cases, the property under the laws of the HOA declaration will prevent a new owner from renting the newly-purchased property for a fixed period of time, which can vary anywhere from six months to three years. Typically, a declaration of condominium document is around 100 pages long, and lists all rights and restrictions of the property and owners of the properties. In addition, there may be modifications or revisions to the document with additional clauses that restrict rental timeframes. It's a common error for investors to rely on the O&E search alone if REO-to-rent is the primary exit or investment strategy. You must conduct a search with the correct title product, something called CC&Rs (covenants, conditions and restrictions).

I know of an example where the investor bought a property at a real estate auction and rented it out to a tenant. A month after the tenant moved in, the attorney representing the HOA sent a violation notice to the investor's mailing address, as well as the tenant's new home, claiming a condominium declaration violation and requesting fines and penalties, as well as removal of the tenant. After removing the tenant and breaking the lease, the investor flipped the property, suffering a huge loss. ProTitleUSA was hired after the fact to determine where the error occurred. If the full state statute search had been ordered with CC&Rs, we found, the examiner would have been able to verify the rental restrictions and the entire situation would have been avoided.

## Issues with Affordable Housing

As an investor in notes, you always have additional considerations to review in the chain of title. For properties falling under affordable housing or 55-plus communities, you need to consider a number of unique restrictions. The sale of these properties is governed by regulations known as the uniform housing affordability controls. These regulations are state-level laws that are tied to the land under these types of properties for their entire period of existence. Every property transfer must be approved by the housing administration, and no sale shall be completed unless approved, including a foreclosure sale. No refinancing or modification can be completed, either, unless approved by the housing agent. Finally, the occupant of each property must be the owner, with the property being his or her principal residence.

# CHAPTER TWENTY-TWO

# HOW TO PROTECT YOUR PORTFOLIO AGAINST TAX SALES

When you purchase a large loan pool, the key to loan preservation is automating the process of calculating the remaining time you have to pay off the taxes. The evaluation of time to go from a tax certificate or tax delinquency to a tax deed should take a number of things into account: the due diligence time cycle, settlement and closing, boarding the loan with the server and, possibly, recording an assignment into the investor's name. It's also a good idea to allow for the kickback of assets that have been lost to tax deeds right after closing, or a certain period after closing, in your reps and warrants agreement with seller. Remember, in many states, the mortgage is completely wiped off by a tax deed without redemption, which then becomes an unsecured asset.

Property or mortgage portfolio managers or servicers for large asset (or mortgage) pools might not notice that one of their properties is going up for a tax sale, or could miss when the taxes and tax certificates are ignored or unpaid. In fact, a few jurisdictions don't require the sheriff or treasurer to even notify all the interest holders of the tax sale. Proactive monitoring of taxes is sometimes performed by servicers, but not always with enough thoroughness to guarantee a property won't be sold at a tax sale. For example, the city of Philadelphia does not require the treasurer to send out notices to interest holders or loan servicers. This practice (or lack of practice) is problematic for title insurance companies when issuing title insurance on the tax deed; lenders who miss the tax sale are forced to file for an appeal, which may lead to a significant expense for the title company.

Every state has unique tax fiscal years (different from the current year), as well as unique installment and due dates. For example, if the current tax year is 2017, Connecticut may be in fiscal tax year

2015, California may be in 2016-17 and Pennsylvania in 2017. There are many online references that can help you with state-specific due dates and fiscal years. In some states/counties, there are additional tax jurisdictions collecting taxes which have the right to foreclose on properties for tax non-payment. States such as Tennessee, Georgia, New York and Pennsylvania have township or city tax jurisdictions collecting taxes separately from the county taxes. In some cases, when the property overlaps two counties, both counties may collect the taxes or one county will collect for both. As an investor, therefore, it's always important to verify the following:

1. The tax card or tax printout has a breakdown of collecting jurisdictions through the county treasurer
2. School taxes are collected through the county
3. The property lies in the township jurisdiction disclosed on the assessor's printout

In many cases, the tax assessor will state on the assessment card that the town code will be county or unincorporated, which means the county collects the local taxes for the township, or there are no township taxes present.

One relatively new Pennsylvania law worth mentioning: As of 2014, any delinquent property tax assessment which has been reduced to a judgment constitutes a lien on all the real property owned by the borrower/owner. A judgment for real estate taxes, once indexed in the prothonotary's judgment index (in Pennsylvania, this is similar to a civil court judgment recording), shall constitute a lien upon all real property of the owner in that county. Therefore, tax liens must be verified for any and all properties the owner owns in this state (which is not very practical, if you ask me).

# CHAPTER TWENTY-THREE

## CURING COMMON TITLE DEFECTS

One of the challenges in the real estate investment business, whether notes or properties, is that each property may pose a new issue or problem that you, as the investor, will need to solve. This makes it difficult to create a consistent pipeline in your investment workflow, as well as a predictable ROI. However, there are a few common cases we see daily while running title reports for ProTitleUSA clients, so I will share a few of these problems, as well as some of the resolutions.

## Dual (HOA and Mortgage) Foreclosure in Florida

In Florida, it's common to see a dual or parallel foreclosure on a condo or apartment. This means the lender and the HOA are filing for foreclosure on the same property, but in different foreclosure actions (different cases). Typically, HOA foreclosures run through courts faster than mortgage foreclosures. The quickest foreclosure I've seen was six months, from the time the HOA lien was filed to having the certificate of title in the HOA's name (the same as a foreclosure deed in Florida). The reason an HOA would file for foreclosure is to pay off all the past-due HOA liens and collect on attorney fees. However, in Florida, when a successful bidder buys an HOA lien at a foreclosure auction, the title is subject to the existing mortgages and other junior encumbrances.

Furthermore, if the foreclosure filings are properly prepared naming the HOA as a defendant, there is a limit to the amount the association can collect from the primary lien holder – 12 months of association fees or 1% of the mortgage, whichever is less.

For the HOA lien investor, this may be a good thing, especially when the sum total of the outstanding liens is less than the market value of the property. In the current market, however, most properties are still underwater. Therefore, it would not make sense for the purchaser of an HOA lien to pay off the existing mortgages. At the same time, a common scenario is to simply rent the property back to the previous owner or a new tenant until the bank finally "comes calling." At that point, you can either walk away or negotiate with the lender. In many cases, to make sure negotiations are successful for all parties involved, the lender will even pitch in tenant relocation money.

Superior liens or not, when an HOA lien is paid off at a foreclosure auction, the successful bidder owns the property, subject to the inferior lien holders. Since these would be paid off, they cease to be a lien and, therefore, are no longer superior. Plus, you cannot put a lien on something you now own, so the money used to purchase the lien is gone. The investor purchasing HOA liens must be working some sort of settlement angle, have figured a way to delay mortgage foreclosure, or have inside information that allows him or her to manage risk by inserting a renter.

For note investors or lenders, the recommended strategy is to settle with the HOA before the HOA forecloses on the property, avoiding the clouded chain of ownership and unclear rights to the property altogether. In the case where the certificate of title is recorded in any sequence by both the HOA and the lender through the separate foreclosure actions, a settlement or negotiation must take place to make one of the foreclosing parties file a rescission of certificate of title. In other words, a cancellation of foreclosure is required by one of the parties. In fact, if the lender has a pending sale transaction with the buyer to pay off the HOA lien instead of the lender, a reinstatement of the HOA lien could be filed.

## More on HOA Liens

Taking a big step back, there are around 350,000 HOAs in the U.S., and around 20% of the homes in those associations are in delinquency. In order to recoup all those delinquent dues, HOAs will not hesitate to place a lien on the property. As you can imagine, HOA liens are very common.

According to servicer reports, on a home with a super lien (see the super lien states table at the end of chapter 8), the average hit for the mortgage servicer is $7,300. In super lien states within your portfolio, investors must act as soon as an HOA lien pops up against the property.

A 2014 HOA ruling in Nevada states that liens held by HOAs take precedence over first trust deeds. Furthermore, an HOA doesn't need to go to court for permission to seize a property, which it is then able to sell at auction for owed assessments and fees. In one related case, US Bank lost an $874,000 first position mortgage! Before incurring losses based on HOA super liens, investors must take steps toward mitigating the issue, including:

1. Proactively monitor (run updates) every three to six months to catch HOA liens before foreclosure.

2. Name the HOA in the foreclosure (do your homework on addresses!).

3. Negotiate and pay off the HOA lien before the foreclosure to preserve its position as the first lien holder.

4. Deliver notice to the lender (required in most super lien states – not Florida), and make sure the servicer's or investor's correct address is on the assignment of mortgage.

### Second Position Mortgage Recorded in first Position in Error

Here's another common problem: The borrower takes out two mortgages during a purchase transaction (or refinances a first position mortgage) without subordinating the position with the previously-recorded mortgage that's supposed to be in the second position.

And here it is with some added detail: When the borrower bought a house while taking out two separate mortgages (a very common practice from 2000 to 2007), the lender or title company sent the deed and both mortgages to the county recorder. The documents were prepared accurately and both were accepted for recording right away. But if the title company didn't provide any instructions to the recorder as to which order to record the mortgages, you have a 50/50 chance of getting the mortgages recorded correctly. All too often, due to title company error, the second position mortgage is mistakenly recorded in the first position.

In a similar example of sloppy document handling, if the first position mortgage was refinanced, but then recorded after the older, second position mortgage, the subordination agreement must be filed together with the refinanced new mortgage to preserve the new mortgage as a first position lien. Often, if the first position refinanced mortgage is through the same lender as the previously filed second lien, the subordination agreement is not even filed. The lender simply skips the subordination agreement filing, causing future issues.

Then, years later, when the first and second position mortgages get sold and assigned to other parties, it can become a serious problem. In this case, the new first position note holder must negotiate a subordination agreement with the second position mortgager to cure the wrong order of liens. For many second position lien holders, this scenario is very beneficial, as the second lien holder is placed in the driver's seat; for their part in curing the defect, they are able to ask for a substantial settlement from the first position lien holder.

The lesson: As a part of your title due diligence, if the first position lien is recorded after the second, always verify the presence of the subordination agreement.

# CHAPTER TWENTY-FOUR

## FORECLOSURE DEFENSE: BORROWER CONTESTED

We will now discuss one of my favorite topics: foreclosure defense.
When borrowers are in default on mortgage payments, some may try
a number of interesting techniques to fight off foreclosure action by
the lender, or delay the foreclosure process. It's all about gaining a
better negotiation position with the lender. Any time a borrower
decides to dispute a foreclosure, it's a last-ditch effort to stay in the
property, and they're willing to do whatever is allowed by our legal
system. With that in mind, as an investor, when you acquire a note,
you have to have your ducks in a row. You need to be sure that there
are no known loopholes that the borrower can dispute in the
foreclosure process. Here are some of the most common arguments
used by borrowers to challenge a foreclosure action:

## The MERS Argument

In an ideal world, the MERS (Mortgage Electronic Registration
Systems, Inc.) system allows you to freely trade and securitize
mortgages under the MERS system or MERS umbrella while, at the
same time, avoiding any conflicts of loan numbers between different
lenders or originators in note sales. One can think of MERS as a
system that assigns a unique identifier – called a MIN (MERS
identification number) – to each mortgage in order to track the
trustees, investors and servicers for each individual loan. The MERS-
originated loan would be identified by MERS verbiage on the
mortgage and note document, as well as a unique MIN on the
mortgage document. In the case of the MERS mortgage, MERS serves
as nominee for the lender that originates the mortgage. Any
assignment or satisfaction of the original mortgage would have to be
signed by the MERS employee or a MERS-authorized signor.

The argument that the borrower can make is based on this question:
"Can MERS have the power to assign or release a mortgage while

being a nominee for the lender?" MERS was deposed on a number of occasions and, from a legal perspective, MERS does not own any interest in the property or the mortgage, and cannot release or assign a mortgage. At the same time, if MERS operates as a nominee for the lender (represents the lender), it can release the mortgage.

After the 2008 crash, most lenders changed their strategy and would no longer release or foreclose on any properties in the name of MERS. In most of those cases, lenders assigned all the mortgage interests for defaulted properties out of MERS, and into the investor or lender having an interest in the note. Due to all the document preparation and recording fees lenders would incur, it's impractical to transfer all the MERS mortgages out of MERS. Therefore, the assignment out of MERS would only be done in the case of default by the borrower.

For investors and lenders, any MERS assignments in the chain of assignments must be examined not only from the assignment document, but also from the signor perspective. MERS must publish a corporate resolution to declare a list of individuals as authorized signors for MERS, in whatever capacity. The signor may be the VP of Documentation, Assistant Secretary, Assistant Vice President or an Authorized signor. If the signor signs as an attorney for MERS, a limited power of attorney must be referenced or present in the county in order to grant power for the signor to sign the document.

I will discuss the additional MERS issues in the sections below. In summary, less than 1% of borrowers dispute foreclosure action by lenders, and only a handful are successful with the MERS argument. In fact, there is a lot of case law precedent in favor of the lender or MERS that allows MERS to be the assignor on assignment documents or releases.

## The Standing Challenge

One of the most common arguments used in court takes place when the borrower challenges the plaintiff's standing. If you don't have proper standing, you cannot be the party foreclosing on a property.

From the prior MERS discussion, a borrower may conclude that if the party identified as the lender is not really the party that loaned the money, the note is defective and probably can't be used as evidence of your obligation. If the note is defective, the mortgage is defective, as well, since it refers to the note. A defective mortgage or deed of trust renders the obligation unsecured.

The loan is the obligation that occurs when the borrower accepts the money or benefits from the funding of a loan. This money is then owed to the entity that actually funded the loan. In conventional loans, before the securitization era, this entity was simply the bank that closed on the loan. Now, the question of who owns the obligation has been heavily obscured. Judges make a distinction between owning the loan (which allows the owner of a note to foreclose) and being the actual creditor (which is the person or entity that actually advanced the money). This question is increasingly in litigation. As more judges take a closer look at the documents, they see that the creditor is not the foreclosing party. This has great legal ramifications in terms of the enforceability of the mortgage or deed of trust. It may even mean that, even when the note accurately describes the transaction, the property might not be subject to foreclosure if the assignment chain is broken or there are visible defects. Additionally, if the note is not a part of the collateral during the note sale, the borrower may argue that the plaintiff does not have a true and original note and, therefore, has no right to foreclose.

## Notary Issues on Assignment of Mortgage (or Deed of Trust)

Notary rules state that the signor must be present for notarization. Also, if there is no date beside the signature, the date of the document is taken as the date of signing. Verify each assignment for notary violations, and see if the signature date of the signor is the same date as the signature of the acknowledgement of the notary. If they are different, get ready to see a motion to produce a notary log with the exact entry of the notary in reference to this transaction, as well as a notary deposition. One would also need to verify whether the notary's commission was expired at the time of the signing.

## QWR – Qualified Written Request

A QWR is a request for production of an original note signed in blue ink. To mitigate this argument, verify that the seller has a copy of the original note and all endorsements.

## Securitization and SEC Issues

About 96% of all residential loans are claimed to have been "securitized." This was intended to mean that the loans were collected into large pools of loans, then divided into smaller pools that were given names like "ABC Asset-Backed Securities Trust 2007-100." The smaller pools were supposedly real estate mortgage investment conduits (REMIC) entities which, under the Internal Revenue code, meant that if they operated in strict compliance with the REMIC code, the pool would not be considered a taxable entity and the tax consequences would flow through to the owners of the pool.

Documents were prepared to memorialize this intention, like a pooling and servicing agreement. In order for the pool to claim ownership of a loan, it needed to satisfy another criterion: it had to exist as a separate entity under the laws of the state in which it was created (usually New York State). Plus, for the claim of ownership to be real, the pool had to be the receiver of the delivery, which needed to be done within 90 days of the loan closing (thus providing a cut-off date that appears to have been consistently ignored by the securitization parties).

As has become clear in court cases and news reports, in most cases, these transfers did not occur in a timely fashion, if at all. Therefore, the lender that appears in the property records – someone who loaned you the money – was actually a paid actor pretending to lend you the money. The documents identifying these entities (like MERS) did not describe a real transaction. Since no attempt was made to transfer the actual obligation to the pool, the claim of ownership appears to be invalid. This has a large legal impact on the ownership of the loan, whether the loan was secured or it was really securitized. It also has a large impact on the identity of who would meet the legal definition of a creditor. This, in turn, would or could negate the ability of any of the present companies seeking foreclosure to actually foreclose on a property. In fact, it could negate any past foreclosures and prevent any in the future.

# CHAPTER TWENTY-FIVE

# PORTFOLIO RISK EVALUATION

Typically, when evaluating large portfolios, each asset would be analyzed from a risk grade perspective. Assuming the final population of assets is nailed down, with some assets being kicked out and replacements added, each of the assets that are left would represent properties that have a mortgage attached and are secured against the property. In addition, the due diligence should report all the issues of each asset. Some issues will be instantly curable, and some issues will be more complex. With nonperforming loan (NPL) trades, it's expected that each asset might have an issue or defect that will require some level of curative action.

Below, I will assign risk grades to assets with different levels of title defects using the 1 to 5 grading system, where 1 is the best/most favorable asset in terms of risk and 5 is the worst.

## *Grade 1*

This is the grade I would give to a clean asset that may only require a payment of delinquent taxes.

## *Grade 2*

Whenever you have an asset with many liens or judgments that could potentially impact the position of the mortgage, or force the investor to execute a foreclosure on the property as the only exit strategy, this represents more of a risk. This type of asset could still get a grade of 2 if there is a curative action to release a prior mortgage, which may involve chasing down the prior mortgage holder.

## Grade 3

Assets requiring many curative actions on the assignment chain could represent a greater risk, and would be graded a 3. During the foreclosure action, for example, the borrower may question the standing, which happens rarely, but is a difficult and lengthy process. Assets tied up in a complicated bankruptcy proceeding would be also grouped in this grade category.

## Grade 4

Assets in the grade 4 category would be carrying a heavy load of liens that could supersede the mortgage's position. These would include HOA liens, a clouded chain of title from the out-of-position foreclosures, or properties with municipal/city violations. Disputed foreclosure actions would also pose a risk due to poor or erroneous motions by the plaintiff's attorney. Other issues that would lead to a grade of 5 would be problems with the legal description of the property and vesting issues in the undetermined vesting issue category.

## Grade 5

Assets that fall into this category of risk would require an immediate action from the lender. This risk category is very broad, and includes (among many other issues) damage to the physical property (like fire damage or unsafe structure violations), property city code enforcement violations with difficult timelines for fixing the issues, an in-progress HOA foreclosure, or a pending tax sale.

Building an average risk factor for the portfolio can provide a good measurement for the overall health of the portfolio, as well as some guidance as to the potential costs of curing the risks. In some cases, it makes sense to put grade 4 and 5 risk groups on frequent monitoring, even prior to recording the assignment of mortgage to transfer the ownership into the investor's name. This gives investors the ability to mitigate any serious risks in advance.

# CHAPTER TWENTY-SIX

## BUDGETING AND REVENUE PROJECTION NOTES

Carefully budgeting for future expenses on a portfolio is a must. There should never be a shortage of funds for representation in a foreclosure or for curing defects. To help you estimate next year's budget, I can suggest a few strategies:

- Budget for next year's tax payments across all assets. During the due diligence cycle, you may request that the title company capture the current year's taxes across all jurisdictions (city, school, county, borough and/or village), as well as all delinquent taxes, including tax certificates noting the maximum interest allowed by the state. (In New Jersey, for example, the tax certificate can carry a maximum of 18% interest.)

- Budget to cure title defects. For example, a code violation lien may need to be paid off at face value, or negotiated down; budgeting should be done assuming face value. If the exit strategy is to foreclose on the property, the investor needs to budget for at least $5,000 to $10,000 per asset.

- Budget for gaps. To fix an assignment chain with a filing gap assignment, for example, would cost about $150 to $350.

Ideally, your due diligence provider on the title will deliver the data in a format that makes it easy to categorize the defects and estimate fees for the associated curative actions. If that is not the case, the ProTitleUSA workflow makes it easy for the investor to parse through the data with enough automation.

## Revenue Projection using Due Diligence and Servicing Requirements

Obviously, the primary goal for investing in real estate is to make money. The best way to project your future revenue is to use your due diligence report to help with exit strategy planning – merge any captured data (such as time or length of foreclosure in a given state or county), recording fees, budgetary assumptions and, of course, the historical model on capitalizing and executing each exit strategy. After each deal closes and revenue data is coming back, the financial model should constantly update to capture any new regulations or delays in foreclosure. The foreclosure timelines get updated quarterly on a state-by-state basis, and these need to be integrated into your model. Finally, it's very important to dynamically monitor your portfolio with title updates at least twice a year; you need to verify if there are any new liens recorded against the property or the borrower.

# CONCLUSION

Now that we know each other better, I hope you will take this collection of lessons and tips to heart. Every chapter, every idea and every word is based on more than 25 years of my personal experience doing exactly what you are about to do – investing in notes and related products.

If I have one bit of parting advice, it is to be thorough and conduct every possible due diligence. That way, you will encounter fewer surprises, make better investment decisions and be a more successful investor.

And, of course, reach out to me at ProTitleUSA any time. We look forward to working with you.

Thank you for your attention.

Made in the USA
Middletown, DE
20 September 2023

38721972R00076